THERAPEUTIC RECREATION FOR CHEMICALLY DEPENDENT ADOLESCENTS AND ADULTS:

PROGRAMMING AND ACTIVITIES

by
Agnes B. Rainwater

American Association for Leisure and Recreation
an association of the
American Alliance for Health, Physical Education,
Recreation and Dance

Copyright © 1992

American Alliance for Health, Physical Education,
Recreation and Dance
1900 Association Drive, Reston, VA 22091

ISBN 0-88314-523-5

PURPOSES OF THE AMERICAN ALLIANCE FOR HEALTH, PHYSICAL EDUCTION, RECREATION AND DANCE

The American Alliance is an educational organization, structured for the purposes of supporting, encouraging, and providing assistance to member groups and their personnel throughout the nation as they seek to initiate, develop, and conduct programs in health, leisure, and movement-related activities for the enrichment of human life.

Alliance objectives include:

1. Professional growth and development--to support, encourage, and provide guidance in the development and conduct of programs in health, leisure, and movement-related activities, which are based on the needs, interests, and inherent capacities of the individual in today's society.

2. Communication--to facilitate public and professional understanding and appreciation of health, leisure, and movement-related activities as they contribute toward human well-being.

3. Research--to encourage and facilitate research which will enrich the depth and scope of health, leisure, and movement-related activities, and to disseminate the findings to the profession and other interested and concerned publics.

4. Standards and guidelines--to further the continuous development and evaluation of standards within the profession for personnel and programs in health, leisure, and movement-related activities.

5. Public affairs--to coordinate and administer a planned program of professional, public, and governmental relations that will improve education in areas of health, leisure, and movement-related activities.

6. To conduct such other activities as shall be approved by the Board of Governors and the Alliance Assembly, provided that the Alliance shall not engage in any activity which would be inconsistent with the status of an educational and charitable organization as defined in Section 501 (c)(3) of the Internal Revenue Code of 1954 or any successor provision thereto, and none of the said purposes shall at any time be deemed or construed to be purposes other than the public benefit purposes and objectives consistent with such educational and charitable status.

Bylaws, Article III

ACKNOWLEDGMENTS

HOLLY GUZMAN   A special thanks to my graduate assistant who brought "freshness," inspiration, information, and a great deal of practical experience to this project. She spent many hours helping me develop materials.

BECKY STACKHOUSE   Another special thanks to the person who "organized" the author and the activities. She did an extraordinary job of editing and typing the book.

JOHN RAINWATER   Special gratitude to my husband for his support, encouragement, and infinite patience.

And thanks to all the individuals who have consented to the use of their activities in this book. Many activities included here have been around long enough to be "public domain," and the originator can no longer be designated and/or recognized.

I stand at the crossroads,
The ever-present intersection,
Between happiness and sadness,
Between importance and worthlessness,
Between peace and unrest,
Between my dream and reality.
Are dreams destined to become realities?
Or are my realities but dreams?
Where do I go from here? Which path do I choose?

-- *Brenda Gortney*

CONTENTS

Chapter One

INTRODUCTION

The intent of this book is to serve as a practical guide for therapeutic recreation personnel working with chemically dependent persons, as well as a resource for counselors, social workers, nurses, physicians, and other professionals in gaining insight into the therapeutic recreation (TR) delivery service for chemically dependent (CD) populations. The text assumes that its readers have a general knowledge of leisure and recreation as well as knowledge of drugs and their effect on the body. This book will address TR as a vital component of the rehabilitation process; the characteristics of CD persons that may influence or affect TR programming and leadership techniques; assessment tools; goals; processing; and specific activities within physical fitness/exercise, leisure education, decision making, stress management, family activities, and outdoor recreation.

When using this book as a resource for inpatient and outpatient programs, it is necessary to consider the length of time a person will be in the program. The length of time for inpatient treatment has been reduced due to insurance companies' limits on length of stay and funding. Therefore, the TR person must determine what programs and activities will be most effective within the designated amount of time.

The materials presented in this book can be adapted for handouts for clients and used as lead-ups to an activity, as visual aids, and as worksheets in organizing thoughts and/or ideas.

Overview

Chemical dependency (CD) devastates healthy leisure lifestyles. Substance use usually starts as a social occurrence, in conjunction with other types of activities. It begins with encompassing the person and progresses from being a part of leisure to being the only leisure. The addiction process continues until it involves the family, the work place or school, and society. To overcome this dependency on drugs requires treatment, formal or informal, which can begin at any time.

Therapeutic recreation (TR) is an integral part of this treatment process. TR serves as a focal point for changes initiated in the other components of treatment. It is the laboratory where patients put into action decisions they have made during individual, family and group therapy sessions. Frequently, there is a vast difference between what patients say and what they do. Patients' attitudes, frustration thresholds, patience, problem solving skills, physical skills, and sense of commitment are directly reflected in recreation participation.

Providing leisure services to CD populations is a challenge that can be met by TR professionals. They have the resources and the skills to provide chemically dependent persons with the tools necessary for positive and active involvement within their personal, family, peer, and community environments, which will enable them to develop healthy leisure lifestyles. However, frequently the therapeutic recreation aspect in treatment is overlooked or handled in an insignificant manner. TR personnel need to be included on the multi-disciplinary treatment team. TR is an important component in the recovery process and should work hand in hand with the other treatment modalities toward a balanced team approach.

Terminology

Several terms will be used throughout this book. Therefore, these terms will be defined as perceived and used by the author.

Leisure - Trying to define leisure is like nailing Jello to a tree. It is difficult to contain in a neat little package and it means something different to each person. The author will define her concept of leisure and this concept will be used throughout the book.

Leisure presents itself first as a state of mind, merging itself with our thoughts and emotions. It can occur at any time and involves freedom of choice. Leisure can involve time and activity/experience. However, neither free time nor activity guarantee leisure, but they can be a means to leisure. Leisure can create feelings of creativity, accomplishment, and satisfaction. It can be active, passive, exciting, or very quiet. Leisure is uniquely personal. The attitude a person has toward a personal experience can decide whether it is truly leisure or not.

Leisure can be an important source for enabling recovering CD persons to cope with their situations. Focusing on leisure emphasizes living a quality life and includes pleasure/ fun, relaxation, increased sense of autonomy, shared experiences, and self-expression. Leisure is a means for people to explore what living "one day at a time" and what "living each day to the fullest" means to them.

Recreation is any activity/experience in which a person gets satisfaction. Categories are arts and crafts; aquatics; communication skills; hobbies; games/sports/fitness; dance; drama; music; social; outdoor/nature; and volunteerism.

Therapeutic recreation (TR) is defined as "the process of selection, development, implementation, and evaluation of treatment, leisure education, and recreation participation services based on individual assessment and program referral procedures" (Peterson & Gunn, 1984, p.6).

In dealing with CD populations, TR will be used to facilitate a change in their behavior through constructive activities and experiences which enable them to develop and maintain a healthy leisure lifestyle as well as healthy leisure behaviors. It is a means of facilitating clients' formation of a new self-image in which they see themselves as worthy of love, and of being good persons.

Leisure education is a process focused on the development and acquisition of skills, attitudes, and knowledge related to leisure participation and leisure lifestyle development. It is a lifelong, continuous process. Leisure education has specific and predetermined content which is operationalized into programs.

The four components of leisure education are (1) self-awareness/leisure awareness, (2) leisure skills and interests, (3) socialization/communication, and (4) leisure resources.

Types of Dependency

Drug use is very much a part of our culture. To eliminate the use and/or misuse would require major changes in some of our beliefs and attitudes. Are people willing to make these changes? Not likely!

Our society gears much of its leisure and recreation toward drugs: coffee, coke, cigarette breaks, keggers, tailgate parties, a beer during bowling, a mixed drink while dancing, aspirin for every little twinge, appetite depressants, "uppers," "downers," a "toke," a "fix." Substance abuse devastates healthy leisure lifestyles. Most people take their first substance as a recreational activity during leisure. If the substance becomes an addiction, healthy leisure and recreational activities are abandoned. This chemical dependency not only affects the individual, but peers, family, the work place, and the community.

The chart on the following five pages notes the drug category, trade/street name, physical and psychological dependency, method of administration, and effects produced by the drug.

This book is not meant to educate on drug usage. The chart is included only as an overview of information needed by the therapeutic recreation staff in order to conduct therapeutic recreation with this population.

Characteristics of Chemically Dependent Persons

Chemically dependent people are persons first and then addicts. They have the same human traits and needs as other persons— to be wanted, to be loved, to be accepted, to be good at things. They are manipulators, masters of evasion, and "con" artists (even to themselves). They may become abusive verbally or physically one minute and then when they realize that they have lost control they become charming. They determine what is necessary to control the situation.

Basic fears govern the actions of CD persons. They are afraid not only to give love, but to receive it. Activities that involve communication skills can be introduced to help these persons express themselves, as well as feel part of a group. They are fearful of both success and failure. Activities in which they can have success are very important, but it is also important that they realize that failures or "losing" happen with everyone. Staff members might get involved in an activity in which they do not excel, which demonstrates that they too can fail and at the same time recognize that fact and go on from there.

CD persons fear their inadequacies. They fear rejection and loneliness. These fears are similar to those felt by all people, but they seem to be felt more intensely by the addict. Most of these persons have an extremely poor self-image and will repress or deny their feelings. They need assertive skills, as well as success in activities so they feel better about themselves. Inner hostility and anger often are demonstrated through aggression. The physical energy of anger can be released through physical activity. Punching bags, ping pong, volleyball, or woodworking can be used effectively as a substitute for the actual object of anger. Group discussion, after the activity, can put the feelings into a frame of reference to be used at a later date when these feelings reoccur.

Dependency needs of addicts dictate that they demand an unreasonable amount of a person's time. They manipulate a person into lengthy discussions and demand constant attention during activities. Structuring activities so clients can assist and praise one another meets this need, although this takes planning and patience on the part of the TR staff, and the cooperation of clients.

Text continues on page 9

Controlled Substances
Uses and Effects

DRUGS	TRADE NAME	PHYSICAL DEPEND.	PSYCHOLOG. DEPENDENCE	METHOD OF ADMIN.	POSSIBLE EFFECTS
Narcotics					
Opium	Dover's Powder Paregoric Parepectolin	High	High	Oral Smoked	Euphoria, drowsiness, respiratory depression, constricted pupils, nausea
Morphine	Morphine Pectoral Syrup	High	High	Oral Smoked Injected	
Codeine	Tylenol with Codeine Empirin Compound with Codeine Robitussan A-C	Moderate	Moderate	Oral Injected	
Heroin	Diacetylmorphine Horse Smack	High	High	Oral Injected	
Hydromorphone	Dilaudid	High	High	Injected Sniffed Smoked	
Meperidine	Demerol Mepergan	High	High	Oral Injected	
Methadone	Dolophine Methadone Methadose	High	High-Low	Oral Injected	
Other Narcotics	LAAM Leritine Numorphane Percodan Tussionex Fentanyl Darvon Talwin Lomotil	High-Low	High-Low	Oral Injected	

Continued

4

DRUGS	TRADE NAME	PHYSICAL DEPEND.	PSYCHOLOG. DEPENDENCE	METHOD OF ADMIN.	POSSIBLE EFFECTS
Depressants					
Chloral Hydrate	Noctec Somonos	Moderate	Moderate	Oral	Slurred speech, disorienta-tion, drunken behavior without odor of alcohol
Barbituates	Phenobarbital Tuinal Amytal Nembutal Seconal Lotusate	High-Moderate	High-Moderate	Oral	
Benzodiazepines	Ativan Azene Clonopin Dalmane Diazepam Librium Xanax Serax Tranxene Valium Verstran Halcoin Paxipam Restoril	Low	Low	Oral	
Methaqalone	Quaalude	High	High	Oral	
Glutethimide	Doriden	High	Moderate	Oral	
Other Depressants	Equanil Miltown Noludar Placidyl Valmid	Moderate	Moderate	Oral	

Continued

5

CONTROLLED SUBSTANCES: USES AND EFFECTS, continued

DRUGS	TRADE NAME	PHYSICAL DEPEND.	PSYCHOLOG. DEPENDENCE	METHOD OF ADMIN.	POSSIBLE EFFECTS
Stimulants					
Cocaine	Coke Flake Snow	Possible	High	Sniffed Smoked Injected	Increased alertness, excitation, euphoria, increased pulse rate and blood pressure, insomnia, loss of appetite
Amphetamines	Biphetamine Delcobese Desoxyn Dexedrine Mediatric	Possible	High	Oral Injected	
Phenmentrazine	Preludin	Possible	High	Oral Injected	
Methylphenadate	Ritalin	Possible	Moderate	Oral Injected	
Other Stimulants	Apidex Bacarate Cylert Didrex Ionamin Plegine Pre-Sate Sanorex Tenuate Tepanil Voranil	Possible	High	Oral Injected	

Continued

6

DRUGS	TRADE NAME	PHYSICAL DEPEND.	PSYCHOLOG. DEPENDENCE	METHOD OF ADMIN.	POSSIBLE EFFECTS
Hallucinogens					
LSD	Acid Microdot	None	Unknown	Oral	Illusions, hallucinate, poor perception of time and distance
Mescaline and Peyote	Mesc Buttons Cactus	None	Unknown	Oral	
Amphetamine Variants	2 5-DMA PMA STP MDA MDMA TMA DOM DOB	Unknown	Unknown	Oral Injected	
Phencyclidine	PCP Angel Dust Hog	Unknown	High	Oral Smoked Injected	
Phencyclidine Analogs	PCE PCPy TCP	Unknown	High	Oral Smoked Injected	
Other Hallucinogens	Bufotenine Ibogaine DMT DET Psilocybin Psilocyn	None	Unknown	Oral Injected Smoked Sniffed	

Continued

CONTROLLED SUBSTANCES: USES AND EFFECTS, continued

DRUGS	TRADE NAME	PHYSICAL DEPEND.	PSYCHOLOG. DEPENDENCE	METHOD OF ADMIN.	POSSIBLE EFFECTS
Cannabis					
Marijuana	Pot Acapulco Gold Grass Reefer Sinsemilla Thai Sticks	Unknown	Moderate	Smoked Oral	Euphoria, relaxed inhibitions, increased appetite, disoriented behaviors
Tetrahydrocannabinol	THC	Unknown	Moderate	Smoked Oral	
Hashish	Hash	Unknown	Moderate	Smoked Oral	
Hashish Oil	Hash Oil	Unknown	Moderate	Smoked Oral	

Source: S. Graber (1987). *Drugs of Abuse.* Kalispell, MT: Scott Publishing Co., pp. 16-17.

8

CD persons usually are impulsive and lack self-discipline. They move from one idea or activity to another and seldom complete anything. Impulsiveness and self-discipline can be controlled through activities that require several processes to complete. Crafts that require planning before actually starting, relays that demand waiting for a turn, or a treasure hunt with progressive instructions aid in curbing these characteristics.

The following table notes contradictions between needs, feelings, and behaviors of the CD person. It is difficult to work with these persons because of these contradictions. Through a variety of different activities that can be introduced to meet the needs and feelings, the therapeutic recreation staff can change the inappropriate behaviors and start the process for meeting the needs. This therapeutic recreation process takes a good deal of time, effort, creativity, and patience.

This book contains many different activities to meet these needs. It might be that all the activities won't be successful for each person, but it must be remembered that these persons are individuals and it will require different leadership techniques, along with different activities, to accomplish intended individualized goals.

CONTRADICTIONS BETWEEN NEEDS, FEELINGS AND BEHAVIORS

OF THE CHEMICALLY DEPENDENT PERSON

Needs and Feelings	Behaviors
*Need to be loved and nurtured	*Afraid to give love and receive it
*Need for success	*Fears of success and invites failure
*Need for belonging to a group	*Rejects and feels loneliness
*Need for positive self esteem/ self-worth	*Demonstrates low self esteem, confidence, and insecurity
*Need for honesty to self and others	*Masters of evasion, rationalization and manipulation
*Need for self control	*Lacks responsibility and self discipline
*Need for release of hostility	*Demonstrates verbal and physical aggression
*Need for recognition	*Inappropriate means of getting attention
*Need for help	*Critical and uncooperative with help that is provided
*Need for structure	*Overly compulsive and restrictive
*Need to be trusted	*Not trustworthy
*Need to care for others	*Displays self-centeredness
*Need for freedom	*Dependent upon others to provide
*Need for suggestions	*Non-responsive to suggestions
*Need to be heard	*Lack of appropriate communication skills; sometimes becoming belligerent
*Need for interaction	*Lack of appropriate socialization skills
*Need for support/understanding	*Defensive
*Need for ordinary "touch"	*Rejection through distancing
*Need for intimacy and sexuality	*Sexual inappropriateness
*Need to be treated as an adult	*Displays childlike behavior
*Need for respect and dignity	*Displays arrogance and selfishness

Needs and Feelings	Behaviors
*Need for stability	*Unable to hold a job or maintain a relationship
*Need to feel normal	*Self medicates
*Need for motivation	*Lack of initiative
*Need to clarify values	*Disregard own value system
*Need for decision-making skills	*Impulsive and lacks ability to determine options
*Need for resources	*Lack awareness of resources
*Need for challenge or excitement	*Lacks control and/or judgement
*Need for leisure skills	*Hesitant to explore new activities
*Need for physical health	*Utilizes substances, fails to exercise or eat properly to meet basic needs
*Need for mental health	*Resorts to substance use to cope with problems and life issues
*Need for laughter and fun	*Angry, fearful of enjoying self
*Need for developing skills and interests	*Apathy towards exploring and follow-through

The Twelve Steps

The Twelve Steps work as a therapeutic framework for both alcoholics, and these steps have been adapted by Narcotics Anonymous for persons addicted to drugs other than alcohol. Written in the past tense, they share the experiences of persons with drug addictions and offer an ongoing guide for recovery.

TWELVE STEPS OF ALCOHOLICS ANONYMOUS*

Step 1. We admitted we're powerless over alcohol -- that our lives had become unmanageable.

Step 2. Came to believe that a Power greater than ourselves could restore us to sanity.

Step 3. Made a decision to turn our will and our lives over to care of God as we understand Him.

Step 4. Made a searching and fearless moral inventory of ourselves.

Step 5. Admitted to God, to ourselves, and to another human being the exact nature of our wrongs.

Step 6. Were entirely ready to have God remove all these defects of character.

Step 7. Humbly asked Him to remove our shortcomings.

Step 8. Made a list of all persons we had harmed, and became willing to make amends to them all.

Step 9. Made direct amends to such people wherever possible, except when to do so would injure them or others.

Step 10. Continued to take personal inventory and when we were wrong promptly admitted to it.

Step 11. Sought through prayer and meditation to improve our conscious contact with God as we understood Him, praying only for knowledge of His will for us and the power to carry that out.

Step 12. Having a spiritual awakening as the result of these Steps, we tried to carry this message to alcoholics, and to practice these principles in all our affairs.

Source: Alcoholics Anonymous. (c) 1976. Alcoholics Anonymous World Services, Inc. New York, New York.

Chapter Two

ASSESSMENT TOOLS

Assessment is a vital aspect of the therapeutic recreation process. Julie Dunn noted: "For therapeutic recreation, assessment can be defined as a systematic procedure for gathering select information about an individual for the purpose of making decisions regarding that individual's program or treatment plan" (Peterson & Gunn, 1984, p. 268).

We must be efficient, effective, and practical in collecting information we need to develop and implement a therapeutic recreation plan for each client. Work loads are heavy, paper work is very demanding, and time is limited. Therefore, do not "re-invent the wheel." Get as much information as possible from records. Do not waste time asking questions that have been answered already in the records. Collect only that information needed for TR programs. The assessment tools needed must be developed for each particular program. The profession has many checklists, questionnaires, and other forms for assessment, which can be used or adapted for use with CD populations. However, most take a good deal of time to complete. Therefore, it is suggested that persons look at as many assessment tools as possible, and then develop their own instrument which "fits" the particular needs of their agency.

Collect only the information you need. Get as much information as possible from the chart. Then determine what additional information you need as related to leisure and construct the assessment instrument to get this information.

The elements that need to be included in an assessment are (1) leisure awareness, (2) past leisure pursuits, (3) present leisure pursuits, and (4) needs and interests and socialization and communication levels.

The assessment of this material should result in (1) a patient needs/problem list, (2) past and current activities and interests, (3) treatment goals determined with the client, and (4) plan for meeting these goals. The individualized plan that results from this assessment will be contingent upon the desires of the client, the available programs and staff, and the budget. Keep these factors in mind when developing the plan.

The following assessments may be used in current form or may be used as resources in developing an assessment tool or tools appropriate for a specific program. The Needs Assessment (page 26) was developed in conjunction with the Contradictions Between Needs, Feeling, and Behavior table (pages 10-11).

THERAPEUTIC RECREATION ASSESSMENT
CHEMICALLY DEPENDENT ADOLESCENT

Name: _____

Age: _____

Date: _____

1. Do you have any physical problems?   If so, what?

2. Do you have any brothers or sisters?

3. Describe your living situation:

4. What is the last grade of school you have completed?

5. Have you ever had a job?   What kind?

6. What do you do in your spare time?

7. Have you ever been in any other programs before?

8. Why are you here?

9. What are your strong points?

10. What do you feel is your biggest problem?

11. What can you do to help yourself?

12. What goals would you choose for yourself?

A. ___ Become more independent
B. ___ Get along better with people
C. ___ Improve school/work habits

D. ___ Develop new skills

E. ___ Learn to feel more
        comfortable in groups
F. ___ Make more decisions for
        myself
M. Add your own goal:

G. ___ Learn to handle problems
H. ___ Relate better to adults
I. ___ Develop new interests
        especially for leisure time
J. ___ Be able to express my
        emotions productively
K. ___ Be more comfortable with
        and trusting of people
L. ___ Follow through with decisions
        I have made

Continued

14

13. How can staff help you?

14. Listed below are several types of activities that people do in their spare time. In the space next to each activity, please rate your interest in that activity according to the following scale:

1. I have never tried it and am not interested in trying it
2. I have never tried it, but would like to try it
3. I have tried it and I do not like it
4. I like it and do it occasionally
5. I like it and do it often

___ Auctions/Garage Sales	___ Exercise	___ Photography
___ Auto Repair	___ Fishing	___ Playing musical instrument
___ Backpacking	___ Football	___ Poker
___ Barbeques	___ Fraternal Organizations	
___ Baseball	___ Gambling	___ Puzzles
___ Backpacking	___ Gardening	___ Reading
___ Billiards/Pool	___ Going to Malls	___ Shopping
___ Boating (canoe, speed)	___ Golf	___ Singing
___ Bowling	___ Hiking	___ Skating
___ Boxing	___ Horseracing	___ Skiing
___ Camping	___ Hunting	___ Sunbathing
___ Caring for pets, plants	___ Jogging	___ Swimming
___ Checkers	___ Motocycling	___ Talking on the
___ Church	___ Movies	telephone
___ Collecting (coins, baseball cards)		___ Tennis
___ Computers	___ Music Listening	___ Video Games
___ Cooking	___ Needlework	___ Visiting
___ Dancing	___ Painting	___ Volleyball
___ Driving	___ Parties	___ Weightlifting

Completed by: Date:

CTRS Signature: Date:

LEISURE ASSESSMENT
Recreational Therapy

Please answer the following questions:

		Yes	No
A. 1.	I feel awkward and uncoordinated in physical activities.		
2.	I shy away from group activities.		
3.	When I play games, I feel I have to win.		
4.	I tend to turn on TV when I don't really know what else to do.		
5.	I feel nervous or uncomfortable when I meet new people.		
6.	I am often bored in my free time.		
7.	I don't know what leisure is.		
8.	My leisure involvement generally becomes less physically active during the winter months.		
9.	I have to finish my work before I can play.		
10.	I would like to learn new recreational activities.		
11.	I have used my drug of choice before a social function.		
12.	I feel uncomfortable in situations where there is no alcohol/drugs available.		
13.	My main leisure activity is getting drunk or high.		
14.	At times I use alcohol or drugs as a means to relax and just get away from it all.		

B. Name 5 things you like to do in your free time and the last time you did them:

1.
2.
3.
4.
5.

Circle the above activities that you did while using your drug of choice.

C. Do you have any hobbies? Yes _____ No _____ If yes, please explain.

D. What kind of physical activities do you actively participate in?
_____ None
_____ Team sports: basketball, baseball, football, others
_____ Individual activities: lifting, exercise, running, walking, others
_____ Free play, games, general recreation, others

E. Check any problems that affect your leisure time
_____ physical abilities	_____ money
_____ no interest/motivation	_____ not enough time
_____ no one to do things with	_____ lack of support
_____ using/getting my drug of choice	_____ other
_____ fear of failure	
_____ transportation	
_____ job	

F. 1. I usually spend my free time with my:
_____ family   List family members:
_____ friends
_____ self   Circle the individuals you get high with.

2. How much quality time do you spend with your family?

G. List the people who would support you in your recovery:

H. My idea of fun is:

I. I have a regular program of exercise that I follow.   Yes _____ No _____
If yes, please specify number of times per week. _____
When was the last time you did this? _____

J. Check off the sentence(s) that best describe your feelings about leisure time:
_____ I never had any leisure time.
_____ My leisure time is controlled by others.
_____ My leisure time is divided between personal pursuits and family pursuits.
_____ I look forward to my leisure time.
_____ I do not look forward to my leisure time.

K. How often is the use of your drug of choice a priority over vacations, hobbies or planned recreation?

L. Has your use of drugs/alcohol caused social problems like loss of friends, hobbies and community activities.   Yes _____ No _____

M. What recreational activities give you self satisfaction and/or enjoyment?

N. What would you like to change about your current lifestyle?

O. What can you do to help yourself make this change?

Continued

Please answer the following questions and indicate on the time sheet below.

1. Indicate on the time sheet the hours that you work. Color that area YELLOW.
2. Indicate on the time sheet the hours that you sleep. Color that area BLUE.
3. Indicate on the time sheet the time that you eat and shower. Color that area BROWN.
4. Would the time sheet be different during the different seasons of the year?
   Yes _____ No _____ If yes, what would be different?
5. What do you do in your current leisure time (free time)?

6. What are the days and times when you are the most ...

Day	Time	
_____	_____	Restless
_____	_____	Bored
_____	_____	Lonely
_____	_____	Wanting to use
_____	_____	Depressed

   Now please add to the time sheet.

7. When do you most often use your drug of choice?

	When do you most often use your drug of choice? What day/days of week?
_____ Morning	_____
_____ Afternoon	_____
_____ Evening	_____
_____ Late Evening	_____

   Now please add to the time sheet.

8. What days do you most often use your drug of choice the most?

   _____ Monday   _____ Friday
   _____ Tuesday   _____ Saturday
   _____ Wednesday   _____ Sunday
   _____ Thursday

   Now please add to the time sheet.

9. Where do you most often use your drug of choice?

   _____ at home   _____ in the car
   _____ at work   _____ hotels, motels, etc.
   _____ at parties   _____ friend's house
   _____ at bars, etc.
   _____ other: where? _____

   Now please add to the time sheet

10. What would you like to do with your leisure time (free time)?

11. Changes I would like to make in my time sheet:
    1.
    2.
    3.

12. What changes can I realistically make in the next year?

Please indicate on the time sheet a typical week before treatment.

	Monday	Tuesday	Wednesday	Thursday	Friday	Saturday	Sunday
8 a.m 12 p.m.							
12 p.m. 4.p.m.							
4 p.m. 8 p.m.							
8 p.m. 12 a.m.							
12 a.m. 4 a.m.							
4 a.m. 8 a.m.							

Source: D. Karapetian

RECREATION ASSESSMENT WORKSHEET

Please answer the questions listed below. Your responses will aid us in developing your recreation treatment plan. THANK YOU!

1. Name_____Counselor_____Age___Date_____

2. Marital Status (circle one) Single Married Divorced Separated Widowed

3. Education Level: (Highest Grade Completed) _____

4. What jobs have you held? (Most recent first)
a. _____ b. _____ c. _____
d. _____ e. _____ f. _____

5. Are you currently employed? ___Yes ___No

6. What have you done for fun and relaxation through the years?
_____ _____ _____

7. List your present recreational interests.
_____ _____ _____

8. List any new leisure activities you would like to try. (see list on next page)
_____ _____ _____

9. What kind of music do you like?
___Country/Western ___Rock ___Jazz ___Classical ___Big Band ___Other

10. Have you ever played a musical instrument? ___Yes ___No

11. Your free time is spent mostly with? ___Self ___Family ___Friends

12. How would you assess your funds available for recreation?
___Insufficient ___Limited ___Adequate ___Plentiful

13. Do you have any physical problems which may prohibit your participation in recreational activities? ___Yes ___No If yes, please explain _____
_____

14. How would you assess your motivational level? ___Low ___Moderate ___High

15. How would you assess your socialization level? ___Low ___Moderate ___High

16. Do you feel comfortable with large groups of people? ___Yes ___No

17. Define the term "leisure" in your own words _____
_____

18. What special strengths or talents do you have (arts and crafts, woodworking, leadership, verbal/communication, writing, physical skills, etc)? _____

_____

_____

Recreation service offers many recreational opportunities to meet a wide spectrum of leisure needs. Please check those that are of interest to you.

___Arts and crafts (favorite:_____)   ___Machine assisted workouts
___Badminton ___Basketball ___Bingo   ___Music, listening ___Movies
___Bocce ball ___Bowling   ___Musical performances
___Card games (favorite:_____)   ___New Games (favorite:_____)
___Conversation ___Cooking/baking   ___Party games (favorite:_____)
___Cross Country Skiing ___Dramatics   ___Picnics ___Pool ___Puzzles
___Exercise (favorite:_____)   ___Reading ___Soccer ___Softball
___Fish ___Floor hockey ___Football   ___Spectator sports events
___Frisbee ___Football ___Golf   ___Swimming
___Gardening ___Horseshoes   ___Table games (favorite_____)
___Individual leisure counseling   ___Table tennis
___Jogging/running ___Kickball   ___Tennis ___Volleyball
___Leathercrafts   ___Walking/hiking ___ Writing
___Other (specify:_____)

19. Please check the goals you wish to attain through participation in therapeutic recreation programs.

___Develop leisure interest   ___Increase comfort in social activities
___Develop awareness of leisure resources   ___Reduce hyperactivity
___Improve use of leisure time   ___Develop creative expression
___Experience success learning and   ___Develop leadership skills
   practicing new leisure skills   ___Develop social relationships
___Experience enjoyment in play   ___Improve self-esteem (image)
___Improve body balance and coordination   ___Explore alternatives to present
___Improve muscle tone and physical fitness   lifestyle
___Increase socialization opportunities   ___Improve mood
___Release anger appropriately   ___Lose weight
___Improve international skills
___Other goals:

       1.

       2.

       3.

       4.

Source: John Watson.

LEISURE ASSESSMENT AND INITIAL TREATMENT PLAN

LEISURE ASSESSMENT

Listed below are several types of activities that people do in their spare time. Please put a check mark beside the activities you are currently involved in (prior to hospitalization).

Art, Craft Shows	Gardening	Relaxation/Meditation
Auto Mechanics	Golf	Religious Activities
Barbecues	Growing Plants	Reminiscing
Bargain Hunting	Hairstyling	Races
Baseball	Hiking	Repairs
Biking	Horseback Riding	Sewing
Boating/Canoeing	Hunting	Shopping
Bowling	Ice Skating	Singing
Camping	Jewelry	Skiing
Cards	Jogging	Snowmobiling
CB/Ham Radio	Lawn Games	Spending Time with a
Ceramics	Leather	Special Person
Checkers	Model Building	Stained Glass
Chess	Movies	Spectator Sports
Collecting	Musical Instrument	Sunbathing
Specify:_____	Specify:_____	Supernatural
Clubs/Organizations	Music/Radio Listening	Swimming
Concerts/Plays	Museums	Table Games
Conversation	Needlework	Teaching a Skill
Cooking/Baking	Painting	Television Watching
Crocheting/Knitting	Parks	Tennis
Dancing	Parties	Video Games
Dating	People Watching	Visiting
Dining Out	Pets	Volleyball
Dramatics	Photography	Volunteer Work
Drawing	Ping Pong	Walks
Education	Playing with Children	Weaving
Electronics	Pottery	Weight Lifting
Exercise	Politics	Woodworking
Family Activities	Pool	Writing
Fishing	Puzzles	Yardwork
Football	Racquetball	Other _____
Furniture Refinishing	Reading	Other _____

What new activities would you like to learn or pick up again?

_____

_____

Continued

LEISURE ASSESSMENT AND INITIAL TREATMENT PLAN, continued

1. What sparks an interest for you? Place a check mark beside not more than <u>five</u>.

trying new things	competing with self or others
being physically active	having something to show for my efforts
being spontaneous	having mobility to come and go freely
doing things at home	getting approval for what I do
helping people	spending time with those close to me
relaxing and taking it easy	having structured and planned free time
being with people	doing things to improve myself
being alone	having fun, laughing and enjoying

2. Do you have any physical problems? _____ If so, what? _____

3. Are you able to afford the activities you most enjoy? _____

4. I have _____ hours a day for leisure.
   This is   Not enough   Sufficient   Too much. (Circle one.)

5. What are your strengths/skills? _____

6. What do you feel is your biggest problem? _____

7. What can you do to help yourself? _____

8. What goals would you choose for yourself? Put a check mark beside <u>two</u>.

Become more independent	Learn to handle problems
Get along better with people	Develop new interests for leisure
Be able to take care of my needs	Be able to express my emotions poroductively
Develop new skills	Be more comfortable and trusting of people
Learn to feel more comfortable in groups	Follow through with decisions I have made
Participate in drug free activities	Feel better about myself
Make more decisions for myself	Be able to stand up for myself

9. Add your own goal: _____

INITIAL TREATMENT PLAN

Based on the goals indicated above and additional problem areas identified as follows:

_____

the Recreation Therapy staff recommendations/goals for treatment include:

_____

_____

Therapist's signature _____

Patient's signature _____

Source: Recreation Therapy Department, Chelsea Community Hospital, Chelsea, MI.

LEISURE ASSESSMENT

COMPLETED BY: _____ DATE: _____

YOUR HOMETOWN: _____ AGE: _____

1) What were your leisure, social and recreational activities during the past few months? (Include all activities, even activities that may or may not involve alcohol or drug use.)

	Activities	How Often? Weekly or Monthly	(1 = low 10 = high) Level of Satisfaction	Level of Performance	Date of Last Involvement
a.	_____	_____	_____	_____	_____	_____
b.	_____	_____	_____	_____	_____	_____
c.	_____	_____	_____	_____	_____	_____
d.	_____	_____	_____	_____	_____	_____

2) What are some of your leisure, social or recreational activities that you no longer participate in?

	Activities	Reason for Stopping	Level of Satisfaction	Age of Last Participation
a.	_____	_____	_____	_____
b.	_____	_____	_____	_____
c.	_____	_____	_____	_____
d.	_____	_____	_____	_____

3) Are you interested in establishing a regular physical fitness program?

___Yes ___No ___Maybe

4) What type of program do you have or would you be interested in establishing?

Explain: _____
_____
_____

5) Do you prefer to exercise ___Alone? ___With Others?

Continued

LEISURE ASSESSMENT, continued

6) Do you have any physical or other limitations that might interfere with your recreational exercise program? ___Yes ___No   If yes, please explain:
_____
_____

7) Describe a typical weekend for you: _____
_____
_____
_____

8) Please list any crafts or hobbies you are presently involved in: _____
_____
_____

9) What activities or hobbies are you interested in that you have not tried? _____
_____
_____

10) Do you spend leisure time with your family? ___Yes ___No
Describe the activities you do with your family: _____
_____
_____

11) What do you do to relax? _____
_____

12) What prevents you from participating in leisure activities? _____
_____

13) Are you satisfied with your present leisure skills and your activities of interest?
___Yes ___No
Please explain: _____
_____

14) Have you had past involvement with Alcoholics Anonymous, Narcotics Anonymous, Cocaine Anonymous, or a spiritual program? ___Yes: number of hours weekly_____   ___No

15) How much time weekly would you like to spend in the above? _____hours weekly.

16) Do you feel depressed? ___Yes ___No

17) Do you like to be with other people?
___All of my free time ___Some of my free time ___Rarely in my free time

18) Do you notice less involvement in your recreational interests when you are "using" substances? ___Yes ___No

19) Do you notice less involvement in social activities when you are "using" substances?
___Yes ___No

Continued

20) Are your main social relationships also your main "using" partners?
____Yes ____No

21) How would you describe the qualities of your social network? (Check all that apply)
____Supportive
____Good Friends
____Caring
____Angry with Me
____"Using" Partners
____ Other (describe) _____

22) Do you belong to any clubs, bowling leagues, church groups? (Please describe)
_____
_____

23) Do you feel you have the "freedom of choice" in your recreational activities?
____Yes ____No

24) What is the average amount of hours you work and/or attend school? _____

25) How much money are you willing to spend on your recreational activities per week?
_____

26) Which statement is most correct about yourself?
____I don't have enough free time ____I have enough free time ____I have too much free time

27) Have you used alcohol or drugs to:

Be more "sociable"   ____Yes ____No ____Sometimes
Reduce "shyness"   ____Yes ____No ____Sometimes
Feel more "playful"   ____Yes ____No ____Sometimes
Give me "courage" to take risks ____Yes ____No ____Sometimes
To feel "relaxed"   ____Yes ____No ____Sometimes
To change my "mood"   ____Yes ____No ____Sometimes
To help express "feelings"   ____Yes ____No ____Sometimes

28) How many years until you retire? _____

29) Have you done any planning for retirement? _____
_____
_____

30) How do you feel about retirement? _____
_____
_____

31) What recreational facilities are available in your community? (for example YMCA, library, skating rink, etc). _____
_____
_____

Continued

LEISURE ASSESSMENT, continued

32) How often have you used community recreational facilities in the past year?
    ___Have never used   ___13-20 times
    ___1-2 times   ___20 times or more
    ___3-12 times

33) What are your leisure and recreational goals?

_____
_____

What change would you like in your present leisure involvement?

_____
_____

34) What do you feel you need from the Recreational Therapy staff to help you?

_____
_____

- STOP HERE -
(Please return this form to Staff - Thank You!)

TO BE COMPLETED BY THERAPIST:

Patient needs/problem list: _____
_____
_____
_____

Interests/life experiences (capacities and deficiencies): _____
_____
_____
_____

Recreational Therapy treatment goals: _____
_____
_____
_____

_____   _____
  Therapeutic Recreation Staff   Date

Pat O'Dea-Evans, from *Leisure Education for Addicted Persons Workbook*, © 1990 Pat O'Dea-Evans, Pea Pod Publications, Algonquin, IL.

NEEDS ASSESSMENT

Circle the number that best represents your feelings on the subjects listed for both the right side and the left side columns.

To Me This Need Is: To Me This Need Is:

very important			not important				being met		not met	

5 4 3 2 1	Need for belonging to a group	5 4 3 2 1
5 4 3 2 1	Need for intimacy	5 4 3 2 1
5 4 3 2 1	Need for success	5 4 3 2 1
5 4 3 2 1	Need to be loved and nurtured	5 4 3 2 1
5 4 3 2 1	Need for positive self-esteem/worth	5 4 3 2 1
5 4 3 2 1	Need for honesty to self and others	5 4 3 2 1
5 4 3 2 1	Need for self-control	5 4 3 2 1
5 4 3 2 1	Need to be trusted	5 4 3 2 1
5 4 3 2 1	Need to care for others	5 4 3 2 1
5 4 3 2 1	Need for freedom	5 4 3 2 1
5 4 3 2 1	Need for help	5 4 3 2 1
5 4 3 2 1	Need for suggestions	5 4 3 2 1
5 4 3 2 1	Need to be heard	5 4 3 2 1
5 4 3 2 1	Need for recognition	5 4 3 2 1
5 4 3 2 1	Need for interactions with others	5 4 3 2 1
5 4 3 2 1	Need for support/understanding	5 4 3 2 1
5 4 3 2 1	Need to give and receive "ordinary touch"	5 4 3 2 1
5 4 3 2 1	Need for decision-making skills	5 4 3 2 1
5 4 3 2 1	Need for structure	5 4 3 2 1
5 4 3 2 1	Need to be treated as an adult	5 4 3 2 1
5 4 3 2 1	Need for respect and dignity	5 4 3 2 1
5 4 3 2 1	Need for stability	5 4 3 2 1
5 4 3 2 1	Need to feel normal	5 4 3 2 1
5 4 3 2 1	Need for motivation	5 4 3 2 1
5 4 3 2 1	Need to recognize and practice own values	5 4 3 2 1
5 4 3 2 1	Need to release hostility	5 4 3 2 1
5 4 3 2 1	Need for resources	5 4 3 2 1
5 4 3 2 1	Need for challenge and excitement	5 4 3 2 1
5 4 3 2 1	Need for leisure skills	5 4 3 2 1
5 4 3 2 1	Need for physical health	5 4 3 2 1
5 4 3 2 1	Need for mental health	5 4 3 2 1
5 4 3 2 1	Need for laughter and fun	5 4 3 2 1
5 4 3 2 1	Need for developing skills and interests in recreational activities	5 4 3 2 1

After completing this assessment, look at the scores on the left of the needs and the score on the right. Are these scores the same within one number of each other? If not, that may be an area of concern for you, or an area which needs attention.

© 1991 H. Guzman

FAMILY LEISURE ASSESSMENT

Please complete the following assessment as a family unit.

1. As a family, do you spend time together in leisure activity?
    ____ yes ____ no

    If yes, how many hours per week?
    _____

2. In the past two months, what activities have you as a family participated in together?

    _____

    _____

    _____

3. Did you enjoy the activity time together? Why or why not?

    _____

    _____

    _____

    _____

4. Do you feel spending some family time together is important? Why?

    _____

    _____

    _____

    _____

5. How could you change the time spent with family to be more positive?

    _____

    _____

    _____

    _____

FAMILY QUESTIONNAIRE

1. What are your family's major strengths? List things that make your family unique, worth belonging to, such as accomplishments, values, attitudes, abilities, traditions.

    _____

    _____

    _____

    _____

    _____

    _____

    _____

2. How can your family life be improved? List problems to be resolved, attitudes to be developed, activities you'd like to try, projects that should be started or finished.

    _____

    _____

    _____

    _____

    _____

    _____

    _____

3. What are your goals? List some goals for the coming year. Make them realistic and specific. Involve your family in goal setting.

    _____

    _____

    _____

    _____

    _____

    _____

    _____

Chapter Three
GOALS

Program Goals

The existing behaviors and attitudes of addicted persons provide guidelines for activity programming. These should be a constant basis for establishing TR goals and objectives for individualized and group programs. Program goals should include the existing behaviors below:

1. To provide concrete means for each individual to set and achieve goals.

2. To provide opportunities to enhance and develop self awareness and self-esteem.

3. To provide opportunities to develop appropriate social interaction and communication skills.

4. To provide opportunities to develop skills and interests to enhance individual leisure lifestyle.

5. To provide opportunities to develop a personal awareness of leisure.

6. To provide opportunities to develop an awareness of and utilize self, peer, family, and community resources.

7. To provide opportunities to participate in mental and physical activities which promote development of a wholesome and enriching leisure lifestyle.

8. To provide opportunities to promote family interaction and involvement.

9. To provide opportunities to clarify values and develop decision-making skills.

10. To provide opportunities to develop stress management skills.

11. To provide and promote opportunities for community outings.

12. To provide incentive and motivation for establishing a satisfying and fulfilling drug-free leisure lifestyle.

Individual Goals

Recovering CD persons must learn to use their leisure time in constructive, positive, and meaningful ways in order to develop and maintain an enriching and quality leisure lifestyle. In order to accomplish a meaningful life they must set and achieve goals. Goals include improvement of self-esteem; increasing self-confidence and self-respect; increasing positive self-regard and self-love; developing leisure interests and skills; clarifying values; and finding appropriate resources and support systems. There are endless choices of activities/experiences to be utilized in accomplishing these goals.

Chemically dependent persons, as well as other individuals, must assume the responsibility for their own leisure. However, much can be done to enhance a healthier attitude toward leisure. Setting realistic individual goals and achieving these goals is one of the basic components in therapeutic recreation. It is important to put these individual goals in writing. "If not in writing, it didn't happen."

The difficulty in shaping and molding leisure lifestyles for an addicted person is the fact that chemical dependency has been the lifestyle of the person, so the entire lifestyle needs to be reshaped/restructured. Providing appealing and acceptable alternatives for use of leisure time is imperative, so the clients must set goals and discover activities that will help in meeting their goals. Each individual must be involved in determining his or her goals. Goals should offer a challenge, but be practical and realistic enough to help the individual develop a leisure lifestyle that is suitable.

Program goals are dependent on the facility, budget, staff, and clientele. Goals must be flexible and adaptable to current demands and circumstances. Goals should be set for the overall therapeutic recreation program and also for each individual program.

It is important to be realistic in setting goals. Do not set goals so high for the clients that they cannot be accomplished. At the same time, do not set program and leadership goals so high that they cannot be accomplished by the TR staff.

Abstinence is a major goal for all CD persons in inpatient, outpatient, and community programs.

> Abstinence can be an end in itself — at first.
> However, recovery involves reliable new opportunities: to contribute, to create, to share, and to appreciate. One must find fulfilling, and not just safe, roles as an individual, and as a member of family and community. (Jackson, 1986 p. 70)

Many of these opportunities and needs can be accomplished through recreational activities.

A POTPOURRI OF INDIVIDUAL GOALS

LEISURE GOALS:

To develop my own philosophy of leisure
To value leisure as an integral part of my life
To put leisure in my daily life
To look forward to activities/experiences
To change the everyday routine
To be challenged/motivated
To be mentally stimulated
To feel fulfilled
To feel less guilty about "playing"
To eliminate barriers, real or imagined, to my leisure

PHYSICAL GOALS:

To be more active
To improve my physical fitness
To burn up energy
To stay in shape/control weight
To develop sport/game skills
To reduce feelings of stress through activity and relaxation

SOCIAL GOALS:

To enjoy social interaction
To make social contacts which will continue in the future
To have fun playing with others
To be with friends
To meet people
To strengthen old friendships and build new friendships
To share a common bond with others like me
To be more humorous and spontaneous

INTEREST GOALS:

To seek opportunities to discover and try new things
To develop new interests
To learn a variety of new skills
To seek further education, formal and informal
To develop assertiveness skills
To study self-improvement techniques
To be involved with family and community

Adapted from: Witman, Kurtz, & Nichols (1987), *Reflection, Recognition, Reaffirmation.*

LEISURE ACTIVITY SELF-CONTRACT

I want to achieve the following goal:

_____

What could keep me from reaching this goal?

____ I don't have the skills, ability, knowledge
____ I don't want it badly enough to work for it
____ I'm afraid that I might fail
____ I'm afraid of what others might think
____ Others don't want me to reach this goal
____ The goal is too difficult to accomplish
Other reasons: _____

What are some things I could do so the above things don't prevent me from reaching my goal?

_____
_____

Who can help me?

_____ Name
_____ Kind of help

What are my chances for success?
____ Very good   Why do I feel this way?
____ Good   _____
____ Fair   _____
____ Poor   _____
____ Very poor

What are some of the good things that might happen?

_____
_____

What are some of the bad things that might happen?

_____
_____

What are the chances that the bad things would happen if I reached the goal?
____ Very high   What could be done to reduce
____ High   the odds?
____ 50/50   _____
____ Low   _____
____ Very Low

Do I still want to reach this this goal?
_____ Yes
_____ No
_____ Still undecided

What are some of the first steps I could take to reach this goal

_____
_____
_____

What else might I do if I am really to succeed?

_____
_____

AM I REALLY GOING TO TAKE THE ABOVE STEPS?
____ Yes
____ No
____ Still undecided

If my answer to the above is yes, I make the following self-contract:
I, _____
 have decided to try to achieve
the goal of _____.

The first step it will take to reach this goal will be to:

_____
_____

by_____

Signed:_____

Date:_____

Witnessed by: _____

Source: P. Earle (1981), *A Leisure Education Notebook for Community Alcohol Programs.*

ONE DAY AT A TIME

There are two days in every week about which we should not worry, two days which should be kept free from fears and apprehensions.

One of these days is <u>Yesterday</u>, with its mistakes and cares, its faults and blunders, its aches and pains. Yesterday has passed forever beyond our control. All the money in the world cannot bring back yesterday. We cannot undo a single act we performed; we cannot erase a single word said. Yesterday is gone!

The other day we should not worry about is <u>Tomorrow</u> with its possible burdens, its large promise and poor performance. Tomorrow's sun will rise, either in splendor or behind a mask of clouds — but it will rise. Until it does, we have no stake in tomorrow, for it is yet unborn.

This leaves only one day — <u>Today</u>! Any man can fight the battle of just one day. It is only when you and I have the burdens in those awful eternities - Yesterday and Tomorrow — that we break down.

It is not the experience of <u>Today</u> that drives men mad — it is the remorse of bitterness for something which happened yesterday and the dread of what tomorrow may bring.

Let us, therefore, live but <u>one day</u> at a time.

Author Unknown

ONE STEP AT A TIME

I. PURPOSES

To gain an understanding regarding the importance of short-term goals in meeting long-term goals.
To gain experience in identifying and writing realistic short-term goals.

II. GENERAL COMMENTS

Short-term goals can be viewed as "stepping stones" enabling one to meet a long-term goal. One way of recognizing progress toward a long-term goal is by acknowledging achievement of short-term goals.

III. POSSIBLE ACTIVITIES

A. 1. Instruct group members to write a long-term goal on the right-hand top lines. The following example may be used: finish high school or GED.

2. Encourage group members to write the first thing needed to be done in order to meet that long-term goal. They should write this in stone #1 (find out where GED classes are held). Proceed to stone #2 (telephone them to get details); stone #3 (pick the best location for me); stone #4 (register); and stone #5 (go to classes and pass the course!).

3. Ask group members to share their example and elicit feedback.

4. Process the value of short-term goals in conjunction with long-term goals.

B. 1. Give one stapled packet of six handouts to each group member.

2. Assign the following categories as goal topics:

a. Professional
b. Personal
c. Financial
d. Social
e. Educational
f. Other

3. Instruct group members to complete one handout per category. Educational goals stated in A (2) may be used as an example.

4. Request that all group members bring the packet back to the group and share them during the next session.

5. Process the value of short-term goals in conjunction with long-term goals.

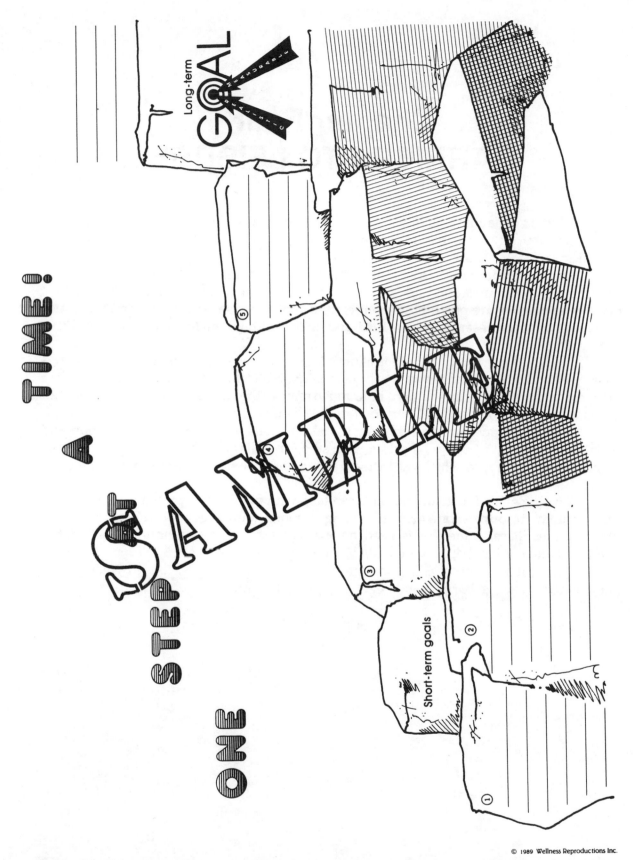

ONE STEP AT A TIME!

Long-term GOAL

Short-term goals

Source: © 1989, *Life Management Skills*. Reproducible activity handouts created for facilitators. Available from Wellness Reproductions, Inc. 1-800-669-9208.

Chapter Four
BARRIERS TO LEISURE

Barriers to having a quality leisure lifestyle are real and imagined. Often times it is not a barrier, but an excuse that keeps a person from getting involved in positive recreational activities.

The most common barriers toward leisure are: negative attitude toward leisure itself, poor communication and socialization skills, poor or lack of recreational skills, inability to plan leisure pursuits, low self-esteem and lack of self-confidence, guilt because they don't feel they deserve to "have fun," and no one with whom to participate in positive recreation.

Addicted persons need to look at their leisure lifestyles and honestly assess what is going well and where changes need to be made. They must look at perceived barriers. Are they real barriers? If so, can solutions be found to remove the barriers? If not, persons should set up achievable goals and get started with the changes.

Informal games are an easy way to help persons overcome communication and social deficiencies. All games, if presented a step (or skill) at a time, can help persons be successful in an activity, which will increase self-confidence and the desire to play the game again.

Writing goals for leisure pursuits can help with planning in problem areas. Identifying human resources can help in finding persons with whom to do activities. As demonstrated here, some things need not be barriers. If the individuals can identify perceived and/or real barriers, they can usually overcome the barriers.

Two different activities are presented on the following pages, to use in helping CD persons acknowledge barriers and begin to cope with them.

INDIVIDUAL BARRIER LIST

List with your counselor or therapeutic recreation staff the leisure barriers that are most significant for you:

Barrier	as evidenced by
1.	
2.	
3.	
4.	

Treatment Goals: Choose at least one treatment goal to correspond with each leisure barrier above:

Treatment Goal Goal Date	Method/Staff Response	Frequency
1.		
2.		
3.		
4.		

_____   _____   _____
   Staff signature   Date   Patient signature

Complete at each two week treatment.
Review Dates: _____

Source: Pat O'Dea-Evans, from *Leisure Education for Addicted Persons,* © 1990, Pea Pod Publications.

BARRIERS

Write an activity on the center of the blackboard. Then ask someone to give one of their reasons for not participating in that activity. Place the response around the named activity barrier.

For example:

Too old

```
┌─────────────────┐
│    Swimming     │
└─────────────────┘
```

Then add other barrier excuses:

No one to do it with

```
┌───────────────────────────────────┐
│                                   │
│    No money                       │
│                                   │
│    ┌─────────────────────────┐    │
│    │    Too old               │    │
│    │                          │    │
│    │    ┌─────────────────┐   │    │
│    │    │    Swimming      │   │    │
│    │    └─────────────────┘   │    │
│    │                          │    │
│    └─────────────────────────┘    │
│                                   │
└───────────────────────────────────┘
```

Next, open the floor for discussion. Ask participants to identify our reason system. The goal is to help participants see how their excuses keep them from participating in activities. Have participants select one item from their ideal list. Have them circle at least three reasons why they don't participate regularly in that activity. Next, have participants generate at least three alternatives and solutions which could help them do the activity they wish to do.

The goal is to have the participants face their excuses and confront them. They generate alternatives to create a way to do the things they really want to be doing.

Source: Pat O'Dea-Evans, from *Leisure Education for Addicted Persons*, © 1990, Pea Pod Publications.

Chapter Five
PROGRAMMING

"To reach the richest harvest in leisure, one must be conditioned and ready for it" (Murphy, 1975, p.159). Programming is extremely important with the CD population. During the initial phase of treatment, activities should be planned which allow persons to feel good, forget about problems, and recharge their batteries. This involves extensive recreation/therapeutic recreation programming. Putting drug-free "fun" into lives is a challenge for the client and for the TR staff.

An ideal inpatient and/or outpatient program would include five week days of structured recreation/therapeutic recreation and two weekend days of planned but informal recreation/therapeutic recreation. During the week there should be 30 minutes of monitored exercises each day, and 1 1/2 to 2 hours of recreation/therapeutic recreation each in the morning, afternoon, and evening. The weekends should include 30 minutes of exercise and then open recreation and planned activities which would include families. The following pages illustrate an ideal time schedule for an inpatient program.

The community recreation/therapeutic recreation programs will vary depending on the economic status of the participants, existing CD programs, budget allocations, and community support. The same categories and activities can be utilized in the community programs.

The idea of daily activity opportunities is an important one. If CD persons are to live "one day at a time," then we must provide treatment and structured activities each and every day. Not only do they need to determine and work on long-term leisure goals in communication, socialization, values clarification, developing new skills, and finding and using resources, but they need interesting and "fun" activities each day.

The overall program should include sessions in the following categories: (1) leisure education: self/leisure awareness, socialization/communication, skills and interests, and resources; (2) activities: arts and crafts, dance, drama/creative expression, music, outdoor recreation, trust games, physical fitness and exercise, and volunteerism; (3) family activities; (4) decision making/values clarification; (5) stress management/relaxation; (6) open recreation; and (7) community outings. Many of the activities included in this book will fulfill several objectives and include different categories.

Leisure Education

Leisure education is extremely important and should be included at least three times a week in both the adult and adolescent programs, as well as once a week for the family. All four components of leisure education should be included.

Activities

Activities cover a broad scope. It is important that there be a variety of activities so that the needs and interests of the individuals are met. The inpatient programs are of such short duration that few new skills can be learned adequately, but persons can get exposed to the activities so they can determine if they want to explore further to learn indepth skills. Each category of activities will be discussed immediately preceding specific activities for that category.

Family Activities

Chemical dependency by one person in the family affects the entire family. Family activities are planned for inpatient, outpatient, home, and community settings. It is important to understand the dysfunctional family and plan activities for the different number of family members, as well as the different age levels. Family activities include not only leisure education, but also family activities that stress "fun."

Decision Making/Values Clarification

Decisions are made every day, but often CD persons do not have the skills to make good decisions. They need to consider choices and alternatives and then be willing to take responsibility for the consequences.

CD persons often cannot recognize or define their own values. They simply have not thought through the value process. The TR personnel can conduct activities which help these persons to clarify their own values, whatever they might be.

Stress Management/Relaxation

We are a stress-oriented society. The important thing is to recognize what causes our stress and then know how to eliminate it. If it cannot be eliminated, then how can it be minimized, and what steps are needed to handle it? Stress management should be offered as a session once or twice during treatment.

Different types of relaxation should be experienced and then the best one for each individual be put in place. Usually relaxation take place just before bedtime.

Open Recreation

Open recreation involves offering a variety of activities during specific times of the day. A person must select something within those activities offered.

Community Outings

Community outings in inpatient programs are usually planned once a week. It is a means of re-integrating persons into the community by exposing them to positive leisure experiences. Only a small number of persons go on these outings. Often times, adolescents must earn the privilege of going on these outings by getting points for good behavior, being in the program for a certain number of days, etc.

It is wise to keep in mind when planning a general range of activities that all activities have potential to be a peak high or low experience for any individual.

40

On this page is a general, overall inpatient schedule and on the following four pages are specific two-week inpatient programs for adolescents and adults. These are suggested programs that can be adapted as needed for your specific population and facility.

INPATIENT DAILY SCHEDULE

Morning:
1. 30 minutes of exercise before breakfast
2. Community meeting - announcements/concerns
3. Medications - set up doctor appointments
4. Group sessions
5. Individual sessions
6. Films
7. Therapeutic Recreation
8. Time to write in diary

Afternoon:

1. Group therapy
2. Individual therapy
3. Films
4. Speakers (addict, staff, recovering CD)
5. Therapeutic recreation

Evening:

1. Group therapy
2. Film
3. AA/NA
4. Family
5. Therapeutic recreation
6. Spiritual/meditation/prayer
7. Relaxation

Weekend:

1. Group therapy
2. Individual therapy
3. Films
4. Family
5. Therapeutic recreation
6. Special events

Therapeutic recreation is the term used for all activities. The author uses only one term, therapeutic recreation, although some authors designate recreation and therapeutic recreation.

INPATIENT - ADOLESCENT
CHEMICAL DEPENDENCY TWO-WEEK SCHEDULE

HOUR	SUNDAY	MONDAY	TUESDAY	WEDNESDAY	THURSDAY	FRIDAY	SATURDAY
6:00 6:30		Wakeup Exercise	Wakeup Exercise	Wakeup Exercise	Wakeup Exercise	Wakeup Exercise	
7:00	Breakfast	Breakfast	Breakfast	Breakfast	Breakfast	Breakfast	Breakfast
8:00		GROUP	GROUP	GROUP	GROUP	GROUP	GROUP
9:00	FILM Indiv. Counsel.	FILM Indiv. Counsel.	FILM Indiv. Counsel.	FILM Indiv. Counsel.	FILM Indiv. Counsel.	FILM Indiv. Counsel.	FILM Indiv. Counsel.
10:00	1. Open Rec 2. Open Rec	Fitness Fitness	Initiative Games Team Sports Table Games	Fitness Fitness	Learn New Skill Learn New Skill	Photography Orienteering Outdoor/ Nature	Open Rec Open Rec
11:00	1. Family New Games 2. New Games	Leis. Ed.: Leisure Awareness Leis. Ed.: Values Clarif.	Stress Mgt. Problem Solving	Leis. Ed.: Self Awareness Leis. Ed.: Decision Making	Nutrition Nutrition	Leis. Ed.: Social Interaction Leis. Ed.: Resources	Nature Walk Outdoor Activities
12:00	LUNCH DIARY	LUNCH DIARY	LUNCH DIARY	LUNCH DIARY	LUNCH DIARY	LUNCH DIARY	LUNCH DIARY
1:00	Open Rec Family Trust	GROUP	GROUP	GROUP	GROUP	GROUP	
2:00	New Games	FILM Indiv. Counsel.	FILM Indiv. Counsel.	FILM Indiv. Counsel.	FILM Indiv. Counsel.	FILM Indiv. Counsel.	
3:00	1. Open Rec 2. Open Rec	Assertive Training Assertive Training	Arts & Crafts Hobbies Arts & Crafts Hobbies	Swimming Indiv. Sports Swimming Indiv. Sports	Community Outing/ Speaker Community Outing/ Speaker	Outdoor Recreation Outdoor Recreation	Family Informal Games Family Informal Games

INPATIENT - ADOLESCENT
CHEMICAL DEPENDENCY TWO-WEEK SCHEDULE
(continued)

HOUR	SUNDAY	MONDAY	TUESDAY	WEDNESDAY	THURSDAY	FRIDAY	SATURDAY
4:00	1.Informal Games	Creative Express.	Arts & Crafts Hobbies	Swimming Indiv. Sports	Community Outing/ Speaker	Outdoor Recreation	Open Recreation
	2.Informal Games	Creative Express.	Arts & Crafts Hobbies	Swimming Indiv. Sports	Community Outing/ Speaker	Outdoor Recreation	Open Recreation
5:00	OPEN REC	OPEN REC	OPEN REC	OPEN REC	OPEN REC	OPEN REC	OPEN REC
6:00	DINNER	DINNER	DINNER	DINNER	DINNER	DINNER	DINNER
7:00	AA/NA Family	AA/NA	AA/NA	AA/NA	AA/NA	AA/NA	AA/NA
8:00	Sing-a-Long Music	Outdoor Activity Table Games	Informal Games	Family Leisure Education	Informal Games	Table Games Informal Games Tournament	Theme Party
9:00	Open Recreation			Family Fun			
10:00	Relaxation Free Time	Relaxation Free Time	Relaxation Free Time	Relaxation Free Time	Relaxation Free Time	Relaxation Free Time	Relaxation Free Time

INPATIENT - ADULT
CHEMICAL DEPENDENCY TWO-WEEK SCHEDULE

HOUR	SUNDAY	MONDAY	TUESDAY	WEDNESDAY	THURSDAY	FRIDAY	SATURDAY
6:00 6:30	Wakeup Exercise	Wakeup Exercise	Wakeup Exercise	Wakeup Exercise	Wakeup Exercise	Wakeup Exercise	
7:00	Breakfast	Breakfast	Breakfast	Breakfast	Breakfast	Breakfast	Breakfast
8:00		GROUP	GROUP	GROUP	GROUP	GROUP	GROUP
9:00							
10:00	1. Open Rec 2. Open Rec	Fitness Fitness	Initiative Table Games Team Sports Table Games	Fitness Fitness	Learn New Skill Learn New Skill	Photography Orienteering Outdoor/ Nature	Open Recreation Open Recreation
11:00	1. Family New Games 2. New Games	Leis. Ed.: Leisure Awareness Leis. Ed.: Values Clarif.	Stress Mgt. Problem Solving	Leis. Ed.: Self Awareness Leis. Ed.: Decision Making	Nutrition Nutrition	Leis. Ed.: Social Interaction Leis. Ed.: Resources	Nature Walk Outdoor Activities
12:00	LUNCH	LUNCH	LUNCH	LUNCH	LUNCH	LUNCH	LUNCH
1:00	Open Rec Family Trust						
2:00	New Games						
3:00	1. Open Rec 2. Open Rec	Assertive Training Assertive Training	Arts & Crafts Hobbies Arts & Crafts Hobbies	Swimming Indiv. Sports Swimming Indiv. Sports	Community Outing/ Speaker Community Outing/ Speaker	Outdoor Recreation Outdoor Recreation	Family Informal Games Family Informal Games

INPATIENT - ADULT
CHEMICAL DEPENDENCY TWO-WEEK SCHEDULE
(continued)

HOUR	SUNDAY	MONDAY	TUESDAY	WEDNESDAY	THURSDAY	FRIDAY	SATURDAY
4:00	1.Informal Games 2.Informal Games	Creative Express. Creative Express.	Arts & Crafts Hobbies Arts & Crafts Hobbies	Swimming Indiv. Sports Swimming Indiv. Sports	Community Outing/ Speaker Community Outing/ Speaker	Outdoor Recreation Outdoor Recreation	Open Recreation Open Recreation
5:00	OPEN REC	OPEN REC	OPEN REC	OPEN REC	OPEN REC	OPEN REC	OPEN REC
6:00	DINNER	DINNER	DINNER	DINNER	DINNER	DINNER	DINNER
7:00							
8:00	Sing-a-Long Music	Outdoor Activity Table Games	Informal Games	Family Leisure Education	Informal Games	Table Games Informal Games Tournament	Theme Party
9:00	Open Recreation			Family Fun			
10:00	Relaxation Free Time	Relaxation Free Time	Relaxation Free Time	Relaxation Free Time	Relaxation Free Time	Relaxation Free Time	Relaxation Free Time

Chapter Six
LEADERSHIP SKILLS

The leader needs to come in with the premise that clients are people first and then addicts. They are individuals with diversified needs and backgrounds. They need the same respect and humanistic treatment that is given to all populations. The addiction should not influence attitude or reaction.

The leadership skills that are practiced with all populations are used with CD clients, with greater emphasis on some areas. Leaders fill many different roles: facilitators, counselors, educators, resource providers, and friends. Leaders need to have the ability to analyze and react to different situations. They must be cheerful, outgoing, relaxed, and secure, enabling them to enjoy themselves honestly, informally, and individually with persons. Leaders should have good personal control, combined with flexibility and adaptability.

Leaders are role models at all times and should behave accordingly. They should participate in all activities, playing with the clients and showing that they are normal by not being skilled in every activity. Clients are delighted when a leader cannot do a skill or "goofs." Clients come in with "negative-isms" which need to be expressed and recognized. Leaders must be empathetic but always aware of manipulation techniques that are used by this population. Understanding, fairness, firmness, and consistency are necessary.

Maintaining group structure is important. Leaders need to take an active part with the CD group to foster and promote formation of good group interactions, socialization, communication, opportunity for feedback, and clarification of ideas and opinions. Groups are designed for promoting success with the activities and also success of interaction and inclusion for each individual. Support groups are very important. They are discussed in Chapter Eleven.

Confrontation

One specific technique used with this population is confrontation. "Confrontation involves facing clients with some aspect of their thoughts, feelings, or behavior that is contributing to or maintaining their difficulties" (Lawson, Ellis, and Rivers, 1984 p. 463). There are two types of confrontation: (1) group, which employs the use of fellow clients initiating confrontation in a controlled session, and (2) individual confrontation, in which a staff member confronts the client without involvement of the group.

Confrontations that are frequently experienced within leisure programs result from negative attitudes toward leisure, leisure participation, and socialization. The TR person should set expectations for behavior. If these limits are not met, a confrontation is necessary.

There are different levels of individual confrontation. The first confrontation usually involves a comment by the therapist that is structured as an observation, followed by a question. For example: "You don't seem to be enjoying yourself. Why is that?" This is followed by more questions that force a person to identify what he or she is experiencing. If the client denies or does not identify what is going on, then a more active confrontation takes place. The questioning technique changes to addressing the client with firm statements towards acting upon the problem. The reason for a confrontation must have a planned purpose involving some positive changes in behavior.

Motivation

A second special technique is motivation. Motivation is that which induces action or determines choice. Initially, when clients come into the program, they experience motivation at the extrinsic level. This includes a point system, a level system, and/or a reward system (re-acceptance by family, peers, workplace, within the social system). Leaders can motivate by encouragement, cultivating hope, and highlighting a client's strengths. In other words, the leader can create a motivating environment in which the CD person can become self-motivated (intrinsically motivated). Ultimately the goal is intrinsic motivation, which includes pride, positive self-concept, feelings of self-worth, and pleasure in leisure.

By recognizing how drugs have affected the different aspects of his/her life, a person can plan for positive changes in behavior, which in itself can be motivational.

Motivation is something that is desired for clients, but it is not always possible. The inability to inspire the desire for change is frustrating for TR personnel. It should be noted that the inability by the client to feel "empowered" to make changes is also frustrating. Motivating is no easy task!

LEISURE ACTIVITY MOTIVATORS

Why do you participate in specific recreational activities? What motivates you to do these activities? Being able to identify "motivators" will be important when you search for activities to substitute for ones you can no longer participate in, or if you simply want to broaden your "recreational horizons."

List your preferred recreational activities. Then, whatever your reasons, or "motivators" (regardless of whether or not they appear on this list), write them next to the appropriate activity.

- to meet new people
- to be with other people
- for the competition
- for the mental exercise
- for the physical exercise
- to increase my knowledge
- to learn new things
- to increase my skills
- to learn new skills
- for a change of pace, variety
- to increase my confidence
- as an emotional outlet
- to share knowledge with others
- to practice old skills
- for fun, pleasure, enjoyment
- to relax, reduce stress
- for sensory stimulation
- to finish something

- to be outdoors
- to share with family/friends
- to be alone, independent
- just for the experience
- to explore new things
- to improve myself
- for the time to think
- for self-motivation, direction
- for distraction
- to confront my fears
- to be creative
- to help others
- to be spontaneous
- to accomplish something
- to keep busy
- to demonstrate skills to others
- to make something tangible
- for the challenge

Activity	Motivator(s)
1.	
2.	
3.	
4.	
5.	

LEISURE ALTERNATIVES WORKSHEET

This worksheet is designed to help you identify some new recreation activities which may provide you with the same kinds of enjoyment and satisfaction as your present recreation activities. Finding such alternatives can expand your leisure horizons, and may help you find rewarding substitutes for activities which have become difficult for you.

In the first column list the recreation activities you included on your Recreation Activity List in Session 1. In the second column list briefly the reasons you have identified that cause you to participate in each of those activities; what motivates you to participate in them. In the third column you will be trying to determine another activity or activities which might satisfy the same set of motivators and give you the same kinds of satisfaction.

Present Activity	Motivators	Alternatives
1.		
2.		
3.		
4.		
5.		

Both activities (pages 48 and 49) are by C. Bullock and R. Palmer, from *Recreation - The Time of Your Life*. Published by the Center for Recreation and Disabilities Studies, UNC-CH. Developed in part with funds from U.S. Department of Education, grant # G008303687.

Processing

Activities with a therapeutic base are designed to promote personal growth, new self-interests and realizations. Sometimes, however, dependent upon the client group, the level of cognitive and self-awareness, as well as the nature of the activity, there is a need for "processing" the activities.

Processing may not always be viewed or even utilized as a necessary component of the activity. The clients' conversations and feedback that they provide during the activity are good indicators as to whether the therapeutic components (or objectives) are being met by the clients. Other indicators such as low levels of client involvement and interests, cognitive abilities, poor attitudes, defensiveness, "horseplay," and low group interactions are determinants in the need for processing.

To communicate and to have the clients learn from the therapeutic basis of the activity remains the prime target for the therapeutic recreator. If understanding why the activity was done is in question, processing needs to take place.

Processing can occur through a series of questions to clients, as well as by the therapeutic recreator drawing upon statements and behaviors made by the clients. Check lists, discussion groups, and having clients evaluate the benefits are also suggested methods of processing. Additionally, processing time should be designed for the intensity level of the activity, the therapeutic intent of the activity, and level of client participation during processing.

Finally, in looking at the processing component within activities, the sole purpose, reason, and idea for its use is not only to meet client objectives, but to give the TR staff opportunity to provide clients with the positive feedback, praise, encouragement, and general self-esteem boosters that many so desperately need. Therefore, to the clients, the element of processing within an activity may be or could have been the best part of the whole activity. Processing should be a part of our therapeutic activities even if it represents something as simple as providing feedback to the clients or something as large as discussing and breaking down the entire activity in a step by step manner.

(Holly Guzman)

Chapter Seven
LEISURE EDUCATION

Most persons spend 13-16 years in school learning how to succeed in a profession/ job. How many classes are offered in leisure? Educating for work is needed, but educating for leisure is also necessary and important. Unfortunately, we are not endowed with leisure interests, values, attitudes, and skills at birth, but must learn them, just as we must learn "job" skills. The importance of leisure education cannot be stressed too strongly. It should be an integral part of our life planning.

Leisure education is a process by which persons learn those skills necessary to develop an individualized quality leisure lifestyle. Leisure education provides the tools that enable a person to understand where, how, why, and with whom to pursue leisure interests and experiences. It enables a person to develop different modes of leisure behavior to adapt to the environment and meet his or her own social and emotional needs. Leisure education can take place throughout life and comes from several different sources: schools, parents, peers, recreation departments, and other human service agencies. Leisure education deals with the individual and the environment. For an individual it encompasses attitudes, values, skills, and knowledge. Within the environment it deals with work ethic, productivity, societal definitions of usefulness as basic criteria for success, well-being, and meaning.

There are four components in leisure education (Peterson and Gunn, 1984. p. 26). For purposes of this book, the terminology has been changed slightly. The four components will include:

1. Awareness
   - self-esteem
   - self-awareness in leisure
   - emotions
   - leisure awareness

2. Communication/socialization

3. Skills and interests

4. Resources
   - support systems
   - self
   - peers
   - family
   - community

Leisure education should be a major part of inpatient, outpatient, and community TR programs. CD persons have a good deal of difficulty with awareness, communication, and socialization. They have limited skills and interests. It is very important that they develop a broad resources base.

Positive attitudes toward the whole concept of leisure are so important. These attitudes affect a person's entire leisure lifestyle. Hopefully, the activities in this section of the book will influence the clients in developing a positive attitude toward themselves as well as toward leisure.

ATTITUDE

The longer I live, the more I realize the impact of attitude on life. Attitude, to me, is more important than the past, than education, than money, than circumstances, than failures, than successes, than what other people think or say or do. It is more important than appearance, giftedness, or skill. It will make or break a company ... a church ... a home.

The remarkable thing is we have a choice every day regarding the attitude we will embrace for that day. We cannot change our past ... we cannot change the fact that people will act in a certain way. We cannot change the inevitable. The only thing we can do is play on one string we have, and that is our attitude ....

I am convinced that life is 10 percent what happens to me and 90 percent how I react to it. And so it is with you ... we are in charge of our ATTITUDES!!!

Charles Swindoll

MY INVENTORY WITHIN LEISURE

Place a check mark next to those statements which best describe you.

1. I like to be alone.

2. I like the outdoors.

3. I enjoy working with my hands.

4. I need to be around other people.

5. I like challenging my mind.

6. I enjoy physical exercise.

7. I would rather stay inside.

8. I like to try new activities.

9. I like to talk on the phone.

10. I like water and water sports.

11. I am happier in cold weather.

12. I would rather be in a warm climate.

13. I like to travel.

14. I can easily find things to do.

15. I like team sports.

16. I enjoy being spontaneous.

17. I am a creative person.

18. I like to construct things.

19. I need to be entertained.

20. I like to test my limits — risk recreation.

What activities can you do to satisfy the statements you have checked? List the activities to the right of the statements checked.

OPEN-ENDED QUESTIONS RELATED TO LEISURE AND VALUES

Complete the following statements.

1. If this next weekend were a three-day weekend, I would select ...
2. My bluest days are ...
3. I've made up my mind to finally learn how to ...
4. If I could get a free subscription to two magazines, I would select ... because ...
5. I feel most bored when ...
6. If I used my free time more wisely, I would ...
7. I feel proud most when ...
8. Socializing offers me a chance to ...
9. If I had no television, I would ...
10. The next rainy day I plan to ...
11. On Saturdays, I like to ...
12. If I had a tankful of gas in the car ...
13. I feel best when people ...
14. On vacations, I like to ...
15. I'd like to tell my best friend ...
16. The happiest day in my life was ...
17. My favorite vacation place would be ...
18. My best friend can be counted on to ...
19. I am best at ...
20. In a group I am ...
21. People who agree with me make me feel ...
22. When people depend on me, I ...
23. I get angry when ...
24. I have accomplished ...
25. I get real pleasure from ...
26. People who expect a lot from me make me feel ...
27. The things that amuse me most are ...
28. I feel warmest toward a person when ...
29. If I feel I can't get across to another person ...
30. What I want most in life is ...
31. I often find myself ...
32. I am ...
33. People who know me think I am ...
34. My greatest strength is ...
35. I need to improve most in ...
36. I would consider it risky ...
37. When people first meet me, they ...
38. In a group, I am most afraid when ...
39. I feel closest to someone when ...
40. I feel loved most when ...
41. I have never liked ...
42. I feel happiest of all when ...
43. When my family gets together ...
44. I like people who ...
45. The trouble with being honest/dishonest is ...
46. Someday, I am going to ...
47. When my friends suggest a leisure activity, I ...
48. I don't have enough time to ...
49. My greatest accomplishment in leisure has been ...
50. My favorite hiding place is ...

Chapter Eight
AWARENESS

Self-Esteem

Self-esteem (self-concept) is the way individuals perceive themselves in relation to the world around them. It is built on feelings of confidence and adequacy, accepting oneself, having some area of achievement, and experiencing certain independence and freedom with oneself. One develops self-esteem by recognition, appreciation, and acceptance by others. Self-esteem has to be nurtured and developed from within the individual and with the help of other people.

CD persons have low self-esteem. They have little confidence, pride, motivation, or self acceptance and feel that they are "failures" in life.

There are many ways in which the TR staff can help persons raise self-esteem. The following suggestions may be helpful, as well as the specific activities presented.

- Find positive points. Decide what you can do well.

- Set your own standards, but realize that no one is perfect.

- Verbalize positive thoughts about yourself.

- Learn to accept compliments from others. Accept them for what they are meant to be.

- Surround yourself with positive people. Get a positive support system.

- Look for the positive in everything.

- Develop and utilize a sense of humor. Laughter and fun are essential.

- Hold up your head and smile. Nonverbal communication is very effective.

Several suggestions and activities for TR staff to use in helping to build self-esteem are presented on the following pages.

WAYS TO BUILD SELF-ESTEEM

1. Let yourself BE YOURSELF.

2. Give yourself permission to "try out" different selves, but don't command yourself to make major changes.

3. Allow yourself to HAVE AND EXPRESS feelings. (You have to feel the lows to enjoy the highs.)

4. Allow yourself to move and grow and change...and to succeed!

5. Allow yourself to take some personal space. And take some personal time. Make dates with yourself. Enjoy your company. After all, if you think about it, no one else is as well tuned into YOUR wants, needs, interests, and desires as YOU are.

6. Give support to others and learn to ACCEPT it in return.

7. Set realistic expectations for yourself. Break big goals into bite-size pieces.

8. Make sensuality a high priority. Re-stimulating your tactile sensitivity can add a new dimension to your life experience.

9. Try new things and allow yourself to make mistakes.

10. Express valid personal wants and needs.

11. Take responsibility for your thoughts, feelings, and ideas by using "IT" messages. It keeps communication lines open.

12. Work on communication skills. Learn to "read" other people, and become more aware of yourself too.

13. Start receiving pleasure, as well as giving it.

14. Accept your body the way it is. That's the first step in changing it.

15. Become more aware of your body image. Visualize what you look like walking into a room. Listen to what you sound like. How do you feel toward other people (rigid, relaxed, etc.)?

16. Say "no" without feeling guilty.

17. Take time EACH DAY to relax. This is a great stress preventer. (And a time saver in the long run.)

18. Become aware of what things are reinforcing you, and use them.

19. Listen to your body. It will tell you all kinds of good things — like when you are hungry, when you are full, when you are tired, when you need to do something active, etc.

20. Allow yourself to fantasize.

21. Visualize yourself with high self esteem. Hear yourself and feel yourself in successful situations.

22. Look UP. The old saying "Things are looking up" actually has some truth to it.

23. Make lists of things you really like about yourself or things that you do well. Ask others to make the same kinds of lists for you.

24. Catch yourself doing things right, and pat yourself on the back.

25. Reframe threats into challenges.

26. Learn to accept compliments.

27. PLAN TO FEEL GOOD.

THE BARKSDALE SELF-ESTEEM EVALUATION No. 69

This Self-Esteem Evaluation measures your current level of self-esteem, your self-esteem index (SEI), and serves as a gauge of your progress in achieving sound self-esteem. It is important to clearly understand all statements and be completely honest in your scoring if you are to obtain a valid SEI. It is essential that you answer these statements according to how you actually feel or behave, instead of how you think you "should" feel or behave.

Score as follows (each score shows how true or the amount of time you believe that statement is true for YOU):   0 = not at all true for me
1 = somewhat true OR true only part of the time
2 = fairly true OR true about half of the time
3 = mainly true OR true most of the time
4 = true all of the time

SCORE   SELF-ESTEEM STATEMENTS

_____   1. I don't feel anyone else is better than I am.
_____   2. I am free of shame, blame, and guilt.
_____   3. I am a happy, carefree person.
_____   4. I have no need to prove I am as good as or better than others.
_____   5. I do not have a strong need for people's attention and approval.
_____   6. Losing does not upset me or make me feel "less than" others.
_____   7. I feel warm and friendly toward myself.
_____   8. I do not feel others are better than I am because they can do things better, have more money, or are more popular.
_____   9. I am at ease with strangers and make friends easily.
_____ 10. I speak up for my own ideas, likes, and dislikes.
_____ 11. I am not hurt by others' opinions or attitudes.
_____ 12. I do not need praise to feel good about myself.
_____ 13. I feel good about others' good luck and winning.
_____ 14. I do not find fault with my family, friends, or others.
_____ 15. I do not feel I must always please others.
_____ 16. I am open and honest and not afraid of letting people see my real self.
_____ 17. I am friendly, thoughtful and generous toward others.
_____ 18. I do not blame others for my problems and mistakes.
_____ 19. I enjoy being alone with myself.
_____ 20. I accept compliments and gifts without feeling uncomfortable or needing to give something in return.
_____ 21. I admit my mistakes and defeats without feeling ashamed or "less than."
_____ 22. I feel no need to defend what I think, say, or do.
_____ 23. I do not need others to agree with me or tell me I'm right.
_____ 24. I do not need to brag about myself, what I have done, or what my family has or does.
_____ 25. I do not feel "put down" when criticized by my friends or others.

_____   YOUR SELF-ESTEEM INDEX (sum of all scores)

TO FIND YOUR SELF-ESTEEM INDEX (SEI), simply add scores of all self-esteem statements. The possible range of your Self-Esteem Index is from 0 to 100. Sound self-esteem is indicated by an SEI of 95 or more. Experience shows that any score under 90 is a disadvantage, a score of 75 or less is a serious handicap, and an SEI of 50 or less indicates a crippling lack of self- esteem.

SELF-ESTEEM ACTIVITIES

I.O.U

Time: 5 - 10 minutes

Use a small group for this activity. It can be used for a birthday party, or a special day for someone in which each person gives that special person an I.O.U. or it can be an activity in which one client selects another client to receive an I.O.U. or it can be used whereby the client offers one or more I.O.U.s for the entire group.

Instructions: The leader talks about the uniqueness of each person and that all people have special skills, whether it be in a sport, creativity, sociability, communication, or humor, etc. Each person is to think about specific characteristics or skills that he or she possesses and is willing to share with others. It cannot be monetary or materialistic. Examples might include: (1) (person skilled in game of tennis.) Give five free lessons of tennis. (2) Share an original recipe. (3) Create a poem for a particular person. (4) Share 30 minutes of sociability together.

Processing: Again the leader will stress the uniqueness of each individual and the fact that each one has so much to offer. Questions: "How did you feel about sharing your skills? Were you surprised at the number of skills that you do have?"

KITCHEN APPLIANCE

Time: 10 - 15 minutes

Use a small group for this activity. Have persons sit in a circle. Everyone is to "think positive!" Discuss the importance of being supportive and looking at different viewpoints. Rules require that there be no negative comments.

Instructions: Address each individual with the following questions: "If you could be a kitchen appliance, what would it be and why?" Let each person respond. If people have difficulty, the leader might use himself or herself as an example: "I would like to be an electric beater because I am always whipping up new ideas and blending people."

IDENTIFY

Time: 5 - 10 minutes

Use a small group. Persons sit in a circle. Everyone is to "think positive!" It is so important that people have positive thoughts about themselves. They can say positive things about themselves. Too often we have been told "not to brag about themselves." We can say positive things without bragging. If we don't blow our own horn, who will?

Instructions: Everyone is to look around the room and find an object with which he or she can identify. Example: "I am like the light bulb. I light up when I see people, I sometimes lead the way, and I am helpful."

Each person then gives his or her examples.

Processing: Were you shy about saying something positive about
                   yourself?
               Did you have difficulty deciding between different
                   objects?
               Did the other people surprise you with their examples?
               Did this exercise make you realize some positive things
                   about yourself?

BRAGS!!

Time: 10 minutes

Get in a circle. Talk about the importance of thinking positive. Discuss how we have been taught not to brag, but also the importance of displaying a positive self-image to others.

Instructions: Each person selects a partner. Give that person three brags about yourself. Then change so the other person "gives three brags."

Processing: Was this difficult to do?
               Did you have difficulty deciding three brags?
               Do you have a positive feeling toward yourself?

I AM GREAT!

Time: 10 - 20 minutes

Each group member creates an ad about themselves, which sells him or her as a "leisurely" person. This can involve a written ad, a visual ad (cut out things from magazines), or a verbal ad. If it is a verbal ad, it should be 30 seconds in length. Before the session starts, the persons should vote on which type of ad they want to do.

Instructions: Each person does this on his or her own. Give about five minutes for them to work on the ad (if visual ad, allow 20 minutes to create). Then have each person present his or her ad.

Processing: Did you sell yourself through your ad?
               Did you communicate well and/or sell your leisurability to persons?

OUR PERSONAL BAGGAGE

<u>Category:</u> Self-esteem/self-concept
<u>Supplies:</u> Brown lunch bags, scissors, magazines, glue
<u>Age Level:</u> Adolescent, adult
<u>Time Required:</u> 50 minutes
<u>Objective:</u> Develop awareness of self as perceived by self and as perceived by others
<u>Description/Instructions:</u>

Each person receives paper bag, scissors, glue, and variety of magazines. Each person cuts out those pictures, symbols, or words that represent the image he or she portrays to others. He or she pastes these images on the outside of the bag. Then he or she cuts out pictures, symbols, or words that represent who he or she "truly is." These images are placed inside the bag.

Each person shares with the group why he or she chose the images on the outside of the bag. Then each person shares the images placed inside the bag.

<u>Processing:</u>   Do you have the same images inside and outside the bag?
If there were differences, what were they? Why do you think they are
different? Do yoｊu try to live up to others' expectations for you?
Do the other clients agree with you? (discussion by others in group)
What would you like to do to change your image? How can this be done?

COMPLIMENTARY SCRABBLE

<u>Category:</u> Self-esteem
<u>Supplies:</u> Basic Scrabble game, paper/pencil (optional)
<u>Age Level:</u> Adolescent, adult
<u>Time Required:</u> 10 - 30 minutes
<u>Objectives:</u>   (1) self-esteem
                   (2) socialization
<u>Description/Instructions:</u>

Complimentary Scrabble is a word game for two people. The play consists of forming interlocking words, cross-word fashion, on the scrabble board. Each word the player forms must be a positive quality of himself or herself, or a word describing a positive quality. <u>Option:</u> You may have player one come up with complimentary words for player two instead of for himself or herself and vice versa.

To begin, each player draws seven letters. The first player combines two or more of his or her letters and places them on the board to read either down or across. He or she then draws to replace as many letters as used.

The second player adds one or more letters to those already played so as to form new words. The blank tiles may represent any letter.

Keeping score is optional. If you decide to keep score, tally the player's score after each turn. The score for each turn is the sum of the score values of all the letters in the word formed. The winning value should be determined before the game is started.

REMEMBER — All words formed must be complimentary to the person himself or herself or to his or her opponent.

THAT WAS THEN, THIS IS NOW

<u>Category</u>: Creative expression
<u>Supplies</u>: Small paper bags
<u>Age Level</u>: Adolescent
<u>Time Required</u>: Varied
<u>Objectives</u>:   To explore self-concept before recovery process began and presently
<u>Sample Goals</u>:   (1) To explore self-image in a creative way
                    (2) To increase self-disclosure to peers
                    (3) To identify own self-image

<u>Description/Instructions</u>:

Give each participant two small sandwich size bags. Ask the group to spend the next 24 hours collecting items that represent aspects of self, before recovery and presently. Items are to be just symbols for self. They can be small drawings or other small items (e.g., "thread -- because I was just barely hanging on ..."). Have participants mark one bag "Then" and one bag "Now."

<u>Processing</u>:

Have group members share their items and tell why they chose them. Process how their self-image has changed -- if it has. This activity is an ending assignment for one group to be processed the next day as a warm up for group therapy.

Source: Pat O'Dea-Evans, ed., *Self Disclosure and Team Building Activities for Chemical Dependency and Prevention Groups*, 1988.

Self-Awareness in Leisure

Each person needs to be aware of his or her personal philosophy of leisure.

- What is the meaning of leisure to you?
- Why is leisure important to you, or is it?
- Are you comfortable in doing activities "outside of work"?
- Are you identified by your "work" or within the "leisure concept"?
- How much of your identity is related to your leisure pursuits?
- Are your values reflected in your leisure?
- What does leisure mean within your lifestyle?
- What gives you satisfaction within your leisure lifestyle?
- Do you play?
- Do your buying habits reflect your leisurability?

The following pages contain some paper and pencil activities that are helpful to persons in perceiving themselves within leisure.

TEN THINGS I LOVE TO DO

Category: Self-Awareness
Supplies: Paper and Pen
Age Level: Adolescent, adult
Time Required: 30 - 45 minutes
Objectives: To identify activities a person really likes
                To identify what is involved in the activities for the individual
Description/Instructions:
      Fill out the following by listing 10 activities you really love to do. Code your list in the following way:

1. Put a dollar sign "$" after all activities that cost at least $3.00 each time you do them. Do not consider initial investment.
2. Put "PL" after all activities that require planning
3. Put an "R" after all activities that involve risk to self-esteem.
4. Put a "B" by all activities that have barriers for doing.
5. Put the date when last done.

ACTIVITY	$	PL	R	B	DATE
1					
2					
3					
4					
5					
6					
7					
8					
9					
10					

Adapted from: © 1972, Simon, Howe, & Kirschenbaum.

Processing: Do you have a broad variety of activities? Are they mostly free?
              Are you spontaneous with your activities or are they planned?
              Is there risk to your self-esteem?
              What are the barriers that would keep you from doing these activities?
              Were most of these activities done recently? If not, why?

LEISURE LIFESTYLE INVENTORY

The following questions have been found to be some of the most useful in aiding a rigorous look at one's leisure style, values, and resources.

<u>Instructions:</u>

This inventory is most effective if you first spend some time in responding. Do some good honest thinking. Your replies could take the form of a diary. You might find initial success by responding spontaneously to each question. This sometimes frees up the mind and later stimulates a deeper reflection. This exercise can uncover a tremendous amount of information which can aid in an understanding of the type of leisure wellness you desire to experience.

<u>The Questions:</u>

1. When do I feel fully alive? That is, what things, events, activities, experiences make me feel that leisure is really worthwhile; that it is great to be doing what I like and want to do?

2. What do I do well in my leisure? That is, what have I to contribute to the life of others; in what skills do I have adequate ability or mastery; what do I do well for my own growth and well-being.

3. What things, relationships, etc. do I think I do poorly while leisuring? What do I (or would I) need to improve upon, if I so desire?

4. Perhaps there are certain habits, patterns of behavior, emotions, or simply things I do in my leisure, but which I would like to stop doing, or at least tone down. (Write these down.)

5. I know there are things or behaviors I would like to learn to do well in my leisure, that is, to feel very self-satisfied in doing. (Write these down too.)

6. Now that I am thinking about it, what do I want to plan to do now, as soon as possible, in my leisure? That is, what are some thoughts, dreams, wishes I have had but now want to do something with ?

7. What are my greatest strengths and assets as a person? What is really going for me?

8. What are my personal weaknesses?

9. Other than my weaknesses, what are some barriers, constraints, obstacles I see possibly in the way of my potential for experiencing high leisure wellness? What risks are foreseeable in trying to overcome such barriers?

10. What deep values in living do I want to realize in my leisure? Do I really believe in leisure enough to believe that I could live out these values?

YOUR HOROSCOPE

A large part of feeling good about yourself is PLANNING to feel good.

This is your chance to outwit your syndicated newspaper astrologer by writing your own horoscope for this month. Begin by writing it the way it has actually gone up to today. Then write it the way you want it to be for the rest of the month. Take it away, Jean Dixon!

_____

_____

_____

_____

_____

_____

_____

_____

_____

Sample horoscope lines:

"August started off slowly with relaxation a high priority."

"Good month for organizing and developing materials."

"Pressure is on, but you make time to relax, recoup."

"Spend more time with family; a good month to get out of town briefly."

"Moon changes on the 20th, and your life takes a turn for the better."

"You're flying high now, all your resources are at your disposal."

"Your creative juices are flowing and you hardly have time to process all your innovative ideas."

LEISURE COAT OF ARMS

<u>Goal:</u> To increase awareness of self within leisure

<u>Time:</u> 30 minutes

<u>Instructions:</u> Fill out the six components by drawing or describing:

Two things you love to do

Two people most influential in your life

The place you had the most positive experience

Two things you enjoy doing with family

Two things you value most

Write three things you would like said about you

After persons have completed the coat of arms, each individual will explain it.

Leisure Coat Of Arms

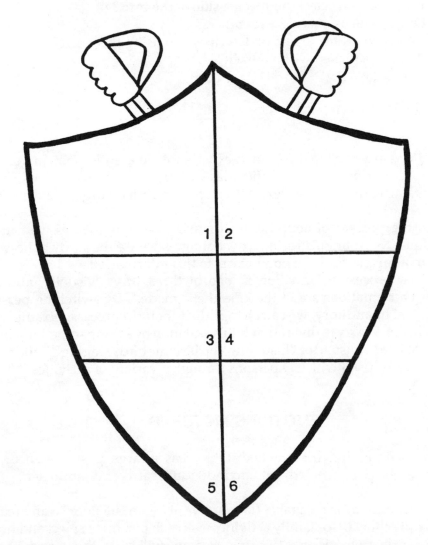

Adapted from: *Leisure Education: A Manual of Activities and Resources,* by Stumbo and Thompson, © 1986.

SELF-AWARENESS ACTIVITIES

<u>Time:</u> 15 - 20 minutes

Each person takes a piece of paper or a 5x7 card. On one side the person writes six words reporting specific facts about himself or herself. Examples: tall, runner, Montanan, parent, reader, gourmet eater. On the other side of the paper, the person writes six words or phrases describing "who" he or she is. These words or phrases must end in "ing." Examples: fun loving, caring, hard working, adventure seeking.

<u>Instructions:</u>
When persons have completed both sides of the paper, they must determine which side they want to share with the group. All people walk around and look at the cards and ask for explanations. Another way to do this is to have one person explain the card to the rest of the group.

<u>Processing:</u>
Why did you select the specific side of the card?
Did you enjoy sharing with others?
Could you think of lots of descriptors in using this exercise?
Are you satisfied with yourself?

Emotions

Six emotions are basic to the human experience: joy, guilt, pain, anger, fear, and frustration. No wonder people have difficulties with their emotions — five of the six are negative. CD persons do have negative emotions and it is difficult to get them into a positive frame of mind.

Through the process of neurolinguistics and psycholinguistics we can assist in changing emotions. Neurolinguistics and psycholinguistics are the study of how the brain processes information and how the body reacts to this information.

Most of us process information in one of three ways: visually, auditorily, or kinesthetically. Our emotions are in the kinesthetic mode. By switching persons from kinesthetic to visual or auditory, we can change their thought process. Example: A child is crying (kinesthetic). We try to divert the child's attention by saying something like, "Look up, do you see that kite?" (visual) or "Listen, do you hear the birds singing?" (auditory). This same technique can be used with CD persons through a variety of activities.

EMOTIONS PICTURES

Wellness Reproductions, Inc. (Beachwood, Ohio) has a large poster with 63 emotion pictures, which can be photo copied, cut into individual cards and laminated.

<u>Instructions:</u> Distribute cards on a table (face up) or place on the floor in an area near the entrance. As people come in for family activities, ask each person to select and hold a card which reflects his or her emotions at this time. Persons will carry these cards throughout

66

activities. Ask the small children to collect the extra cards and give to you (they love being involved).

At the end of the activity period, ask persons to look at their cards to see if they are still experiencing the same emotion. (Usually emotions have become more positive.) They can share the emotions with the group if they want, but it isn't required.

Processing: Did your emotions change? If so, why?
               Did it have to do with activities? Activities can change your moods. It is important to do activities that make us feel positive and elicit different emotions.

GUESS HOW I FEEL

Time: 15 minutes

Instructions: Place cards face down. Each person draws a card and acts out the emotion or discusses the emotion, e.g., What brings on that emotion? What can you do about it?

Leisure Awareness

To be or not to be at leisure . . . that is the question! A person needs to define leisure.

- What is it?
- Is leisure a right or a privilege?
- How does it affect your life?
- What is your leisure lifestyle?
- What needs can you satisfy through leisure experiences?
- What are your current recreational activities?
- Dop you have a wide variety of recreational activities?
- Do you have a satisfying leisure lifestyle?

On the following pages are several activities to help heighten the leisure awareness of chemically dependent individuals.

LEISURE AWARENESS ACTIVITIES

Times I did this last year month week				Times I will do this next year month week		
___	___	___	Went on a tour trip	___	___	___
___	___	___	Attended a movie, concert or play	___	___	___
___	___	___	Played golf or went bowling	___	___	___
___	___	___	Entertained guests in my home	___	___	___
___	___	___	Worked in the garden or yard	___	___	___
___	___	___	Took a long walk for exercise	___	___	___
___	___	___	Attended a religious service	___	___	___
___	___	___	Went out to dinner with a friend	___	___	___
___	___	___	Did some volunteer work	___	___	___
___	___	___	Telephoned or wrote letter to a friend	___	___	___
___	___	___	Went fishing, hunting, or camping	___	___	___
___	___	___	Served on a committee	___	___	___
___	___	___	Played cards, chess, or Scrabble	___	___	___
___	___	___	Tried a new craft, game, or recipe	___	___	___
___	___	___	Went to a party (or gave one)	___	___	___
___	___	___	Exercised or jogged to lose weight	___	___	___
___	___	___	Attended a sports event	___	___	___
___	___	___	Shopped for new clothes	___	___	___
___	___	___	Helped a friend with some work	___	___	___
___	___	___	Read a book or watched a TV special	___	___	___
___	___	___	Added something to a collection	___	___	___
___	___	___	Made something I was proud of	___	___	___
___	___	___	Visited a friend or relative	___	___	___
___	___	___	Played a musical instrument	___	___	___
___	___	___	Went cycling, skiing, or swimming	___	___	___

LEISURE INTERESTS

Instructions: Circulate through the group of people present. Find persons who have done one or more of the things listed below. Once identified, have that person sign your paper. Continue with the list. You can include more than one name for each activity.

FIND SOMEONE WHO ...

1. Has set one goal for learning a new recreational skill after discharge. _____

2. Has decided upon two family activities, and can name them. _____

3. Can name two resources for social gatherings (without drugs and alcohol) in his/her hometown. _____

4. Has a hobby. What is it? _____

_____

5. Participates in some kind of physical activity every day. _____

6. Can name three recreational goals he/she wants to accomplish while in treatment. _____

7. Can enjoy do-it-yourself projects. _____

8. Has initiated a new friendship while at this facility. _____

9. Likes to sing. _____

10. Reads the newspaper daily. _____

11. Likes to dance. _____

12. Doesn't care who is in the World Series. _____

13. Plans to maintain a friendship with a "using" buddy. _____

14. Can have fun when broke. How? _____

15. Honestly enjoys leisure. _____

PIE OF LIFE

Fill in this pie with activities you do during these times. It will include family time, work, recreation, and sustenance (sleep, eat, personal care). Fill out one for weekdays and one for weekends.

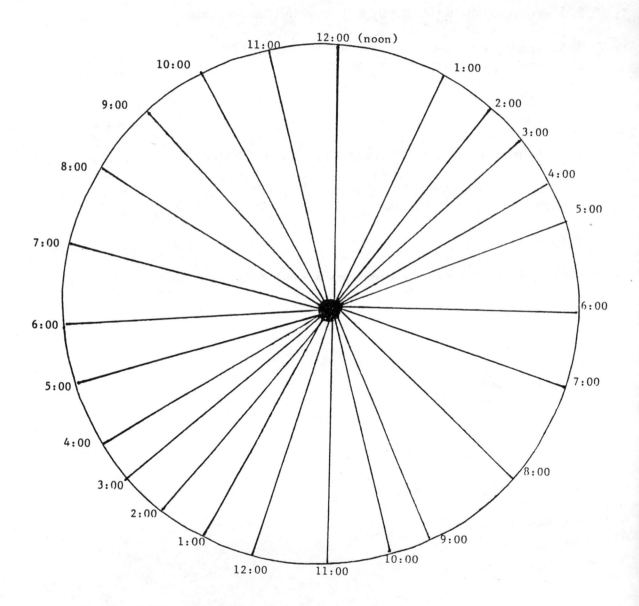

LEISURE CONCENTRATION

Time: 15 - 30 minutes

Print pairs of cards with related leisure terms (an activity and a skill needed to do it, or the equipment involved, etc.). Print the activity on one card and the related activity or equipment on the other. (Be sure to keep a master sheet with the related pairs, in case there is an argument.) Possible card pairs:

Concert - Michael Jackson
Swimming - Bikini
Horseback Riding - Saddle
Camping - Sleeping Bag
Drama - Charades
Baseball - Hotdog

Visiting - Friends
Poetry - Cinquain
Bridge - Cards
Chinese Cooking - Wok
Canoe - Paddle
Relaxation - Daydreaming

Another good way of playing would be to have pictures of things, rather than the words. A good project is for the participants to make up a set of cards themselves. Start with five pairs, and gradually increase to 10 - 15 pairs.

Instructions:
Shuffle the cards and place one-at-a-time face down on the table. Participants take turns turning up two cards. If the cards match the participants keep them. If not they are turned face down on table (in the same position) and the next person takes a turn. If the participant does match the pair, he or she gets to keep the cards, and gets another turn. When all of the cards are gone, each person adds the number of cards he or she has. The highest number wins.

LEISURE CHARADES

Time: 30 minutes

Instructions:
Play the regular game of charades, but use only categories that relate to leisure. It might be wise to begin with a number of slips of paper with activities written on them and hand these out to the teams or individuals.

An alternate way to play the game would be for each individual to act out his or her own favorite leisure activity. Another way is to divide into two or more teams. Each team writes on individual cards ten leisure activities. These activities are put in a bag and one person from another team draws a card. He or she then acts out the leisure activity and own team must guess what it is.

Can put timer for the winner, or can just do it as a fun activity, without competition.

LEISURE PUZZLE

Time: 10 - 20 minutes

Use construction paper. Pre-cut different colors into different shapes (heart, flower, diamond, square, tree). Cut out the shapes to form a puzzle, with enough pieces in each puzzle for each person in the group. Pass a different puzzle out to each group.

Instructions:
Each person in the group takes a piece of the puzzle and writes three recreational activities in which he or she excels or enjoys. Each person then discusses what his or her activities are and why they were chosen. Then the group puts the puzzle together.

Processing: Did you have a variety of activities for each person?
                Did you have a variety of different activities for each person?
                Did you find some common interests?
                Did any activities mentioned by others motivate you to try that activity?

LEISURE POSTCARD

Time: 10 - 15 minutes

Instructions:
Each person in the group draws a picture of his or her ideal vacation. This is perceived as the picture on a postcard. The person then writes a message to whomever he or she wants to receive this card. Each person shares the postcard with the group.

Processing: Did you have one specific vacation that was really special?
                Did this vacation bring back lots of good memories? Not so good?
                Why did you send the card to a specific person?
                What was your message?

LEISURE PLACES

Time: 10 - 20 minutes

Each team brainstorms and lists as many leisure places or leisure activities as possible. Each team then circles only those that everyone in the group has done. Team scores one point for each place/activity listed plus two points for each place/activity in which all team members have participated.

Another way to play is to list all possible leisure activities/places. Then one team starts by calling out each activity on list. If other teams have the activity, then that activity gets crossed off the list. When that team has completed calling off the list, another team starts (calling only those activities not crossed off) using the same procedure. When all teams have called their lists, the remaining activities are counted (one point each), and a winner is determined.

LEISURE COLLAGE

Time: 30 - 45 minutes

Have available: leisure magazines (sports, crafts, outdoor, photography, travel, games, aquatics, etc.), posterboard, scissors and glue. Have participants cut out pictures of activities they enjoy doing or would like to try, and have them make a collage. Then ask them to share with their peers some of the activities they've chosen.

TRAVEL AGENT

Time: 30 - 45 minutes

Therapeutic recreation staff has previously written to state and city travel and tourist bureaus for tourist information packages. Then these are put in large envelopes, one per state. There are also fifty cards, one per state, in a bag. Participants reach into the bag and take out a state, then receive that state's envelope. They then go through the literature and pick out two or three things to do in that state (visit park, amusement center, museum, raft, festival, etc). Then they plan a presentation, pretending that they are travel agents and are trying to sell a trip to that area.

Have a few postcards per participant available so they can write to any places from which they would like to receive information.

This activity could be done interstate as well.

WE'VE DONE IT ALL

Category: Leisure Awareness
Supplies: 3 x 5 cards, masking tape/tacks, list of categories
Age Level: Adolescent, adult
Time: 50 minutes
Objectives: To recall a variety of activities related to specific skills, areas, words
To brainstorm different types of activities
To determine who shares same kinds of activities
To foster teamwork and cooperation
Description/Instructions: Divide group into teams of 4-5 persons. Appoint a runner for each team. Designate an area on the wall in front of each team which will be used to tape or tack cards. Determine end of game by the length of time, or a certain number of categories to be used.

The leader calls out one of the categories listed below. Each team must find one specific activity that all members have done within that category. As soon as leisure activity is identified, the runner writes it on a card, runs to wall and tapes the card facing in. The first team to complete this task gets one point. The rest of the teams must still post an activity if they don't want to lose a point.

The other team may challenge the winners if they do not believe the entire group has done the activity. If the group is challenged, they must prove that all of them have done the activity.

List:

Ice	Water	Snow
Dirt	Sand	Mud
Balls	Wheels	Sound
Paper	Uniform	Cleats
Tennis Shoes	Wood	Group
Pictures	Fruit	Money
Throwing	Kicking	Hitting

(This is only a tentative list. Add categories, or get suggestions from participants.)

Processing: Were you surprised at things everyone had done?
Did it remind you of things you hadn't thought about for awhile?
What about activities listed that you haven't done?
What about barriers for doing these activities?

LEISURE CATEGORY TAG

Category: Leisure Awareness (physical game)
Supplies: None
Age Level: Adolescent
Time: 10 minutes
Objective: To stimulate thought processes regarding leisure while benefiting from exercise

Description/Instructions: This tag game involves having to call out a leisure activity in a specific category just prior to getting tagged in order to stay immune. If an activity can't be named, "it" can tag that person, who then becomes "it."

Someone is selected to be "it." "It" selects any category of leisure; examples: leisure activities done while standing, in the winter, in the sunshine, done indoors, etc. The possibilities of leisure categories are endless. Participants are to run away fro "it." If "it" comes close enough to a person to tag them, that person can name an activity in "it's" Leisure Category and squat. In doing so, that person is immune from becoming "it." If, however, the person can't come up with a leisure activity in "it's" leisure category, or comes up with an improper activity (in case of dispute, game leader will decide), "it" can tag that person, and that person becomes "it."

Processing: Did you have a hard time coming up with leisure categories in a certain category when pressed for time?
Was it hard to remember what category was currently being used?
Can you see the many different activities that you can do in leisure?
What types of activities do you like?

LISTEN

When I ask you to listen to me
and you start giving advice
you have not done what I asked.

When I ask you to listen to me
and you begin to tell me why I shouldn't feel that way,
you are trampling on my feelings.

When I ask you to listen to me
and you feel you have to do something to solve my problem,
you have failed me, strange as that may seem.

Listen! All I asked was that you listen,
not talk or do — just hear me.
Advice is cheap, 50 cents will get you both Dear Abby and
Billy Graham in the same newspaper.
And I can do for myself; I'm not helpless,
maybe discouraged and faltering, but not helpless.

When you do something for me that I can and need to do for myself,
you contribute to my fear and weaknesses.

But, when you accept as a simple fact that I do feel what I feel,
no matter how irrational, then I can quit trying to convince
you and can get about the business of understanding what's
behind this irrational feeling.
And when that's clear, the answers are obvious
and I don't need advice.
Irrational feelings make sense when we understand
what's behind them.

So, please listen and just hear me. And if you want to talk,
wait a minute for your turn;
and I'll listen to you.

Anonymous

Chapter Nine
COMMUNICATION/SOCIALIZATION

Communication

Communications, verbal and nonverbal, are an integral part of our lives. Interpersonal relationships evolve around communication. Communication is defined as "the transfer of meaning from a sender to a receiver" (Bowman & Branchaw, 1988. p. 38) and involves inferences, perceptions, expectations, and intentions.

Sixty-five percent of communication is nonverbal, while 35 percent is verbal. Types of nonverbal communication are (1) physical gestures: raised eyebrows, shrug of shoulders, thumbs up, wave of the hand, push away, wink, cry; (2) physical appearance: looks, clothes, posture; (3) relative position of space: space between persons, space of chairs, park bench; (4) communication of time: late to social gatherings, but not to dinner, if don't care for person do not spend time with them; and (5) control position: stand while others sit, magnitude of gestures.

CD populations have difficulty communicating, either verbally or nonverbally. They have underdeveloped or lost social skills, limited social contacts, and inability to interact with others. Communication and socialization go hand-in-hand. CD persons need to practice verbal communication skills. Initial help by the TR staff in assisting these persons is through informal recreational activities that require some type of communication. Social recreation, informal games, New Games, and drama are categories of recreation which can be used effectively to facilitate development of all types of communication.

Communication activities, involving mainly physical activities and games, are also described in Chapter Seventeen.

HEADBANDS

Category: Communication
Supplies: One construction paper headband for each participant
Age Levels: Adolescent, adult
Time: 20 - 25 minutes
Description/Instructions: This exercise is most effective with groups of 10 to 15 members. In a larger group, a small group performs while the remaining members observe.

One headband for each participant is prepared. The headbands can be made with construction paper cut to fit the heads of the participants. Each headband is lettered to show a particular role and an explanatory instruction as to how other members should respond to the role. Some examples are:

Expert: ask my advice
Comedian: laugh at me
Ignorant person: sneer at me
Important person: refer to me
Loser: pity me
Boss: obey me
Helpless person: support me

The facilitator places a headband on each participant in such a way that the member cannot read his or her own label but other members can see it easily. The facilitator provides a topic for discussion or presents a decision that must be made and instructs the group as follows:

1. Each member is to interact with the others in a way that it is natural for him or her. Members are not to role play, but to be themselves.
2. The group is to react to each member that speaks by following the instructions on the speaker's headband.
3. The group is not to tell each other what their headbands say, but simply to react to them.

After 20 minutes, the facilitator halts the activity and directs each member to guess what his or her headband says and then to take it off and read it. Discussion is then initiated and includes any members who observed the activity.

Processing: What were some of the problems of trying to be yourself under conditions of group role pressure?

How did it feel to be consistently misinterpreted by the group; for example, to have them laugh at you when you were trying to be serious, or to have them ignore you when you were trying to make a point?

Did you find yourself changing your behavior in reaction to the group's treatment of you; for example, withdrawing when they ignored you or giving orders when they deferred to you?

SEND UP THE MESSAGE

Category: Communication
Supplies: 5-10 sheets of paper for each group, one pencil per group, one chair per person
Age Levels: Adolescent, adult
Time: 15 minutes
Objectives: To enhance nonverbal communication skills
To understand that communication also involves touch

Description/Instructions: The group is divided equally into teams who are asked to form single rows. All team members face the same direction and close enough to touch the back of the person in front of them. The person at the front of the line is given the sheets of paper and a pencil. The leader instructs the teams that the last person in each row will be shown the same simple drawing and that this drawing will be sent up to the first person by having each teammate draw with his or her finger on the back of the person in front of him or her. The picture can only be drawn once by each person. When the front person receives the message, he or she will draw it on the paper. Each team drawing is displayed. It is judged by the groups as it is compared to the actual drawing.

Once this is done, the activity continues with the teams rotating their seats until each member has been given the opportunity to draw a picture.

Processing: Did you feel a responsibility to your team in
               receiving and passing the picture?
          Did you feel frustrated?
          Did you feel effective with nonverbal communication?
          Did you feel like part of a group?
          Is this a means of communication in itself?

Holly Guzman

WHAT'S IN A PICTURE?

Category: Communication
Supplies: Magazine pictures that contain several people and objects
Age Level: Adolescent, adult
Time: 15 minutes
Objective: To enhance communication skills

Description/Instructions: Five people are chosen to leave the discussion area, or move to a distance where they cannot view or hear the group.

The group is shown a picture. The activity begins when one person is brought back from the group of five and shown the picture. The person looks at the picture for two minutes trying to remember all details. Once the two minutes are up the picture is covered.

The second person is then asked to enter the room. The first person tells the second person as much as he or she can remember about the picture within two minutes. This process then continues with the second person telling the third person what the first person saw, the third person telling the fourth person what the second person saw, and lastly the fourth person telling the fifth person what the third person saw. At no time during this process can the second, third, fourth, or fifth person talk with the first or break this order.

The activity is stopped when the fifth person describes the picture to the group. The picture is then shown to the group of five to see how accurate their description was.

Processing: What is seen and what is told may vary greatly. What is heard and what is
          told may vary greatly. People have different perceptions of what
          they see.
    Not always is the whole description of the picture communicated. Parts are
          sometimes left out which can cause confusion/misunderstandings.
    People may not always hear the message communicated to them, thereby
          causing misunderstandings.
    It is important to check back with the original sender of the message to
          determine if we are understanding and getting the right message.
    Talking is the best way to clear up issues and problems.

PUZZLE

Category: Communication
Supplies: Picture of puzzle, puzzle pieces
Age Level: Adolescent
Time: 15 - 30 minutes
Objectives: To communicate by verbal instructions only
                    To listen to verbal instructions and follow through
                    To ask questions when instructions are not clear

Description/Instructions: Get a simple puzzle with 25 pieces or less. (Children's puzzles are good, or make your own.) Everyone pairs up. The pairs sit back to back, one person has a picture of the puzzle completed and the other person has the pieces to the puzzle. The person with the picture gives verbal instruction to the other person. The object is to put the puzzle together with just verbal instructions.

Processing: How did it feel not being able to see the person
                        giving instructions?
                What did it feel like to give instructions and not being able to see how the
                        person is doing?
                How did it feel to depend on someone else to complete a task?
                Were you proud to have finished the puzzle?
                Do we all need to develop skills in giving instructions and listening?

CAREER CHOICE

Review the jobs listed below and select one in which you are most interested. Prepare a brief statement describing your qualifications based on your personal characteristics and strengths (do not include degrees, training, etc.). Persons in the group can ask questions after you have "sold" yourself for the job.

1.   Social director on a cruise ship
2.   Insurance salesperson
3.   Park ranger
4.   Counselor at a CD halfway house
5.   Ride operator at an amusement park
6.   Coach for youth sports
7.   TV comedian
8.   Game show host or hostess
9.   Helicopter pilot
10. Computer programmer
11. Recreation leader in a community center
12. Model for "Air Jordan"

Adapted from: *Reflections, Recognition , Reaffirmation*, by J. Witman, J. Kurtz, and S. Nichols, © 1987.

I.D. GRAB BAG

Category: Communication
Supplies: Scissors, magazines, paper bags, colored markers
Age Level: Adolescent, adult
Time: 15 - 20 minutes
Objectives: To communicate non verbally and verbally
        To get to know some of the other group members
        To gain skills in expressing feelings

Description/Instructions: Pass out a magazine, scissors, and a paper bag to everyone in the group. Each person needs to cut out three items from the magazine that he or she feels represents or describes something of himself or herself. For example, one might cut out a pair of tennis shoes because he or she is athletic, or cut out a picture of a safe because he or she feels all locked up inside. When three things have been cut out, they are placed in the paper bag and the tops of the bags rolled shut.

      When everyone has done this, break into smaller groups according to color on the bottom of their sacks. There should be about five or six people to a group. Members of each group will put their bags into the center of the circle they are sitting in and mix them up so they cannot be identified. Each person then takes a bag and opens it up. The object is to try to guess to whom the items belong. Once the person is identified, he or she must explain why items were chosen. After everyone has done this, join participants in large group again.

Processing: Do you feel like you know the people who were in
            your group a little now? Why?
        How do you feel about what you've been exposed about yourself?
        Were you comfortable in talking about yourself?

LEGO LINGO

Category: Communication
Supplies: Lego blocks
Age Level: Adolescent, adults
Time: 20 - 30 minutes
Objectives: To look at ability to communicate, handle stress, and work as a team

Description/Instructions: Leader puts together a Lego sculpture using approximately 3-5 Legos of different sizes and shapes. Figure doesn't represent anything. Two member teams, one the runner and one the builder, are trying to communicate to build an identical sculpture with the runner communicating to the builder how to build it. The builder has the identical pieces, but jumbled in a pile and is about 20 feet away from the original sculpture and a barrier is between the sculpture and the builder so the builder has no chance of seeing the sculpture. Runners look at the sculpture, run to the builder, and give verbal directions to the builder on how to arrange the legos to exactly duplicate the original sculpture, returning to view the original when necessary. Use of hands by the runner is forbidden. When the runner feels sure the sculpture is duplicated, he or she should make one last check, then the team carefully carries its sculpture to the original sculpture to compare it.

Participants may feel that this is a race, but each team continues until all have finished and checked their sculptures.

Processing: Discuss how the runners felt about not being able to simply build the sculpture and about not being able to use their hands to communicate. Ask the builders how they felt about having to rely on instructions from the runners. Discuss if they had any problems, frustrations, or obstacles and how they handled them. Did they come up with any strategies? Talk about how the exercise relates to everyday interactions and how they can apply what they have learned.

Suggestions: The leader might consider glueing original sculpture together so no one accidentally knocks it apart. Leader may also consider making a second identical sculpture so that those carefully carrying their sculpture to check it can go to a different area and not be in the way of those still running to finish theirs.

Adaptations: Use more or less Legos, use different building materials, vary running distance, or have a third teammate who never sees the original sculpture but instead gets directions from the teammate who can see it and communicates those directions to builder.

VISUAL AND VERBAL IMAGES USED IN ADVERTISING

The purpose of advertising, whether for TV, radio, magazines, or newspapers, is to encourage the public to use and buy the product advertised. Thus, advertisers work to make their products appealing and suggest on some level that by using the product the consumers' lives will be better, happier, healthier, easier, or more fulfilling.

Divide into groups of 4-5. Each group gets an ad for liquor. Let them study the ad. For each ad analyze the following elements:

1. Visual images in the ad. If there are people in the ad, what do they look like? (successful, sexy, powerful rich, poor, "together")
   What are they doing? (talking, engaged in an activity, boating, singing)
   How do they appear to feel? (happy, sad, turned on, confident, inviting)
   How are they dressed? (casual, formal, well-dressed, sloppy)
   If there are no people in the ad (only a bottle or a glass of liquor), what feeling does picture suggest? What is the mood of the ad?

2. Written copy in the ad.
   What does the copy tell you about liquor?

3. Total effect of the ad.
   According to the ad, if you like to drink the alcohol, how will you feel? What will you look and act like?

4. Total effect of all ads analyzed.
   What basic similarities do you see in these ads?
   If the ads are to be believed, how will drinking alcohol affect you?

81

MAKING SENSE OUT OF OUR SENSES

Category: Communication/drama
Supplies: Cards with a separate dsilemma written on each one
Age Level: Adolescent, adult
Time: 15 - 20 minutes
Objectives: To become aware of nonverbal and verbal communication skills
To cooperate with each other as peers
To encourage leadership development

Description/Instructions: Two volunteers are selected. One is given a card with a dilemma written on it and is instructed to perform a seemingly easy skit. The dilemma is that one of the two performers has a barrier to "normal" communication. The rest of the group observes but cannot help the two performers. Props can be used, but they are not necessary. The development and refinement of the skit are not important.

Some examples are:

(1) A student must show a new student around the school. The dilemma is that the student is deaf. Nonverbal skills will be used.

(2) A person is asleep in a burning room. Your job is to awaken him and explain the situation. He is a Cambodian and speaks no English.

(3) A blind person is walking across the street. In his path is an open manhole. What skills will be used? Sometimes words are not enough.

Processing: Clients are encouraged to give positive comments about the actions.
What else could have been done to help?
Has anyone had a similar experience that he/she would care to share with the group?
Try to develop your own situation to use at another time.

Modifications: If someone gets stuck, a person from the audience could offer suggestions.

IMPRESSIONS

Time: 10 minutes

Verbal and nonverbal communications give many different impressions. Group sits in a circle. The group decides on a topic area (motels, food, cars, leisure activities, etc.). Each person, in turn, looks at the person to the right and tells him or her a single phrase description from the topic area which explains why he or she chose that phrase. Then the person described is asked if he or she perceives self in that same way.

Examples: Motel - "You remind me of a Holiday Inn--pleasant and give good service."
Food - "You remind me of celery--you are tall and cool."
Cars - "You remind me of a GTO--sleek and sporty."
Recreation - "You remind me of a racquetball--intense and quick."

GESTURES

<u>Time:</u> 15 minutes

Group stands in a circle. All members are asked to think of a particular gesture, mannerism, cue, or signal for self. Each person demonstrates self gesture.

A person is designated as "it." This person first gives his or her own gesture and then gives someone else's gesture. This second person must pick up on the message, give own gesture and then pass the signal on by giving someone else's gesture. If a person fails to pick up on his or her signal, or if unable to pass the signal on, he or she is caught and given a marker. The game then resumes as before. This is a cooperative activity and no one is eliminated.

The game can also be played by passing the signals to the beat of some music.

TELEPHONE

<u>Time:</u> 10 minutes

A group or several groups form lines. The first person in each line is given a story to pass to the next person in line. The story can be told only once to the next person. The story continues down the line. The last person in each line takes turns telling the story as heard by them.

This usually gets a laugh from all concerned, as the story has been changed. After the laughter has stopped, discuss the importance of clear and concise listening and relating.

WEEKLY OUTLOOK

Category: Communication/Socialization
Age Level: Adolescent, adult
Time: 20 minutes
Objectives: To look at the positive happenings of the week
               To analyze problem areas to determine solutions
               To look at support systems
               To plan ahead

Description/Instructions: Each person fills out the sheet as related to self. Group discussion with anyone wishing to participate.

HIGHLIGHTS OF MY WEEK	WHAT COULD HAVE BEEN DONE TO MAKE THIS WEEK BETTER?

WHO SUPPORTED ME THIS WEEK?	LEISURE PLANS FOR THE FUTURE

A HUG FOR ALL REASONS

Category: Communication
Supplies: A "hug" pre-test and poem
Age Level: Adolescent, adult
Time: 15 minutes
Objective: To help break down the wall around the recovering alcoholic so that the lines of communication between the alcoholic and those he or she has harmed in any way can begin to improve as the alcoholic begins to make amends

Description/Instructions: Have participants get into pairs. The leader will introduce the activity and its purpose.

Due to time constraints, only four different hugs will be learned by the participants and the leader will include a narrative with each hug presented.

Hug #1 - A Frame Hug

- participants stand facing each other, arms wrapped around each others shoulders, sides of heads pressed together, bodies not touching below the shoulders
- this is a hello or good-bye hug
- it is good for formal situations because it is not as threatening as the full body hug

Hug #2 - Butterfly Hug

- participants stand face to face
- they bend at the waist and place both arms over each others shoulders but do not touch below the shoulders
- using their hands, the participants pat each other on the back
- this is a "don't mess up my hair, Dahling" hug and also one that could say "you're a good person" as well as hello or good-bye
- once again, it is relatively nonthreatening and good for situations which may be new or uncomfortable

Hug #3 - Side to Side Hug

- participants stand sideways, shoulder to shoulder
- they place one arm around their partner's shoulder and squeeze
- this is an "I'm proud/happy of/for you" or a "it'll be ok" as well as an "I care hug"
- this one gets a bit more personal and can lead to a full-body hug because in a sense, it is a hug which tests the other person's feelings

Hug #4 - Heart Centered Hug

- participants stand with direct eye contact with partner
- they wrap their arms around each others shoulders/back
- their heads are together and there is full body contact
- this is a full, long and caring hug that nonverbally conveys strong feelings between the partners and is a powerful form of touch

Processing: Discussion should follow this activity.

Source: Unknown

HUGS PRETEST

1. Hugging reduces stress.   True or False
2. Hugging is a basic need such as food and water.   True or False
3. Adults love to hug babies.   True or False
4. Before hugging you should get permission.   True or False
5. There are many kinds of hugging that all have their
   own purpose.   True or False
6. The back to front hug was invented while doing dishes.   True or False
7. Zen hugging is a kind of hugging.   True or False
8. Hugging contains no calories, nicotine, saccharin,
   or sodium.   True or False
9. Hugging is natural.   True or False
10. You can hug anyone, anyplace, anytime.   True or False

HUGS

It's wondrous what a hug can do,
A hug can cheer you when you're blue.
A hug can say, "I love you so,"
Or, "Gee, I hate to see you go."
A hug is "Welcome back again,"
And "Great to see you! Where've you been?"
A hug can soothe a small child's pain,
And bring a rainbow after rain.
The Hug! There's just no doubt about it--
We scarcely could survive without it!
A hug delights and warms and charms,
It must be why God gave us arms.
Hugs are great for dads and mothers,
Sweet for sisters, swell for brothers.
And chances are your favorite aunts
Will love them more than potted plants.
Kittens crave them, puppies love them,
Heads of state are not above them.
A hug can break the language barrier,
And make your travels so much merrier.
No need to fret about your store of 'em;
The more you give, the more there's of 'em.
So stretch those arms without delay,
and give someone a hug today!

Dean Walley

Socialization

"No man is an island." We are all social beings. We need other people. We need to socialize. Social recreation is one means of doing just that. It is one of the most delightful forms of recreation, with emphasis on friendliness, sociability, fun, laughter, and such social graces as courtesy, kindness, respect for others, and fair play. It gives immediate pleasure and seeks to entertain. It is doing something just for the fun of it, or a more current saying, "just for the health of it."

Common problems for CD persons are underdeveloped or lost social skills, limited social contacts, and the inability to interact with others. They have either lost social skills during the substance abuse period, or "used" during their social development years and never developed adult social skills. Social/emotional growth ends when addiction begins. For example, if a person is 13 when he or she became addicted and 19 when receiving treatment, he or she remains socially/emotionally at age 13. Therefore, the TR leaders must gear activities accordingly. They must work with the individual to update social behavior and emotional responses. New Games and cooperative games are helpful in integrating the different age levels.,

Social recreation is a mechanism for opportunities in group experiences that meet fundamental needs for social involvement. Social recreation can replace the drug by providing a healthier but equally enjoyable "high."

Social recreation includes mixers, parties, music, dance, eating together, informal games, guessing games, puzzles and tricks, and stunts. A tremendous number of books on social recreation are easily available. Therefore, only a few activities will be noted in this chapter and some activities are included under other sections.

Role modeling of social behaviors by the TR staff is very important. Staff should participate in all activities--playing with the clients, talking with them, going to events, and behaving like friends.

This socialization section is divided into four segments: Fun and Laughter, Social Games, Puzzles, and Speakers, Special Events, Outings. In addition, ice breaker/acquaintance activities, de-inhibitizer activities, and social responsibility activities are described in Chapter Seventeen.

Fun and Laughter

Play, laughter, and humor are important parts of our lives. You can see this in the spontaneous, carefree actions of children, but we have lost much of that playfulness by the time we are adults.

The TR staff should help clients experience laughter, fun, feeling comfortable about enjoying themselves, and recognizing those activities that give them joy and satisfaction. The staff must realize that there is a delicate balance in providing "fun" activities. Some persons perceive fun as "kid stuff" or play (which they perceive as only for children) as "acting silly." Having fun threatens their "cool" image and/or they are concerned that someone might laugh at them.

However, childlike games (note I didn't say childish games) are often helpful in breaking down these inhibitions or fears. Charades, New Games, round songs (e.g., Row, Row, Row Your Boat), and challenging games are examples of activities that can minimize the fear in having fun (or in failing) and in breaking down inhibitions.

Suggestions for enhancing recovery through laughter and play can be found in these statements:

"You are as young as you feel."

"Be young at heart."
"Play a silly game today."
"Children are to be heard laughing."
"That's child play and I want to do it."
"It's only a game and it means a lot."
"No grins, no gains." (Rush, 1991, p. 28)

To achieve a state of laughter, you can use activities such as the following at the beginning of any TR session. Another good activity is the Humor Drama Exercise, which is described in Chapter 14, under Creative Expression.

WHO MAKES YOU LAUGH

Instructions: Divide into groups of 4-5 persons. Each person is to tell the group who makes them laugh and why. It can be a friend, family member, or comedian. After they have talked about their selection, stress the importance of being around people who give you positive feelings, laughter, and fun.

MOVE OVER

Instructions: Circle enough chairs for everyone in the group. Persons are to follow instructions as read by the leader:

> If you haven't had a hug today, move over. (Everyone should move to the left.)
> If you haven't received a smile today, move over.
> If you haven't laughed today, move over.
> If you don't have blue on, move over.
> If you play tennis, move over. Etc., etc.

It is obvious that persons will be sitting on other people's laps, but if someone is sitting on your lap, it is difficult to move over. This situation causes laughter and fun.

POTENTIAL HUMOR ACTIVITIES

1. Expressions/face exercises
2. Humor likes and dislikes activity
3. Favorite forms and performers of comedy
4. Exploration of comedy forms: visual arts, cartoon ing, literature, audio, slapstick, irony, satire
5. Analysis and discussion of forms of comedy exercises: movies, TV shows, comedy albums, comic strips, magazine jokes
6. Humor scavenger hunt
7. Clowning activities
8. Create a humorous collage
9. Humor wish list for daily laughter desires
10. Humor games
11. Humor role playing exercises
12. Pantomime activities
13. Laughing records, laughing figures (Sir Laugh a Lot") or balls, humorous sayings or stories

GET TO KNOW YOUR NEIGHBOR BETTER

Category: Social Games
Supplies: Pens, pencils, paper
Age Level: Adolescent, adult
Time: 15 - 20 minutes
Objectives: To increase and encourage group communication
            To get to know each member of the group better
            To increase awareness of individual differences

Description/Instructions: Arrange group in a circle and have them divide a sheet of paper into five separate sections. Make sure that everyone is writing with the same color of ink, pencil, and paper. Five questions will be asked concerning an individual's preference in a specific subject.

1. What is your favorite recreational activity?
2. What is your favorite color and why?
3. What TV character do you most like and identify with?
4. If you could be an animal, what type would you be and why?
5. Who is your favorite music group and why?

The leader of the group collects the folded responses and keeps them separate in their respective piles. Keep the piles of responses separated and be sure to mix them up well. After all questions have been asked and collected, the leader will mix up the answers in one pile and pass them out to the group. The object then for the group is to guess what answer matches the person who filled it out. If a person receives his or her own answer mix the sheets up again and redistribute.

Variations: Increase the number of questions, or type of questions, and have the participants identify appropriate questions.

KNOW YOUR NEIGHBOR

Category: Socialization
Supplies: Worksheet, pencils
Age Level: Adolescent, adult
Time: 25 minutes
Objectives: To get acquainted with other persons in the group
            To know people by different leisure interests

Description/Instructions: Each person is given a worksheet (see next page). Divide into groups of three or four persons. Persons interview those individuals in their group, answering as many questions as possible. Person writes down information as other person speaks.

WORKSHEET FOR KNOW YOUR NEIGHBOR

Persons are in groups of three or four. Each participant has a worksheet and interviews others in the group. Get answers to as many questions as possible, writing down the information as other person speaks. There are 12 questions, but they do not need to be asked in numerical order.

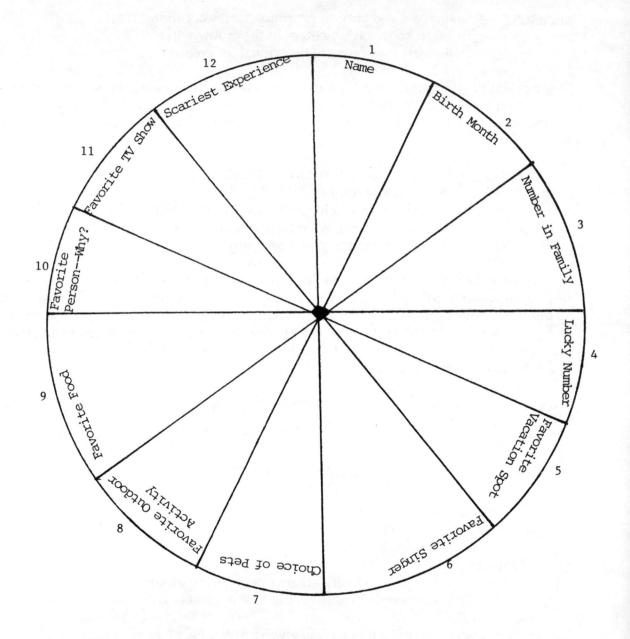

POLAROID SCAVENGER HUNT

Category: Socialization
Supplies: Polaroid cameras, scavenger lists
Age Level: Adolescent, adult
Time: 2 - 3 hours
Objectives: To socialize and have fun
                To be aware of things in the community
                To do something unique and different

Description/Instructions: Divide into groups of four to six. Each group has a camera. Each group is given a scavenger list of 10-15 descriptions for pictures they must take. They must choose five that they can submit within two hours.

Rules: Everyone must be in the picture. At the end of two hours all groups must return and submit pictures to panel of judges.

Points:
    100 - everyone in front of City Hall with the mayor
    100 - everyone at the bowling lane
    100 - everyone doing some type of water activity
    100 - everyone receiving their library card
    100 - everyone at a sports event
    100 - everyone in the back of a pickup with driver
             present
    100 - everyone next to a Corvette
    100 - everyone eating at McDonald's
    100 - each picture over the five required

You can make up your own list ... these are only suggestions.

© B. Artz, National Recreation and Park Association

WHAT IS IT?

Instructions: Form a circle. Pass around an object, with each person demonstrating it as something different. Group has to guess what it is. Example: a pencil = pointer, baton, pool cue, baseball bat, needle, etc.

BALL PASSING

Instructions: Group forms a circle. Pass a ball in a certain sequence. After you have passed the ball, put hand on your shoulder so you won't receive the ball again. After everyone has received the ball, start the same sequence again, but you don't need to put your hand on your shoulder. Go as quickly as possible. Now reverse the sequence.

    After this sequence has been done three times, add several different size and color balls and keep them all going at once.

THIS SHOE HAS A STORY TO TELL

Instructions: Each person takes off left shoe and puts it inside the circle. Each person selects a shoe and tells a story about where that shoe has been. They need to be as creative as possible.

SLOGANS

Instructions: Divide into groups of three to five persons. Make a list of slogans. Make up a quiz for these slogans (five questions). Each group will challenge other groups to answer with correct slogans.

BLACK MAGIC

Category: Confederate game
Instructions: Two persons are cohorts (they know how the game is played). The group members choose an object in the room, while one of the cohorts is outside. When he or she comes into the room the other cohort points to different objects in the room. When the "inside" cohort points to the chosen object, the other cohort correctly identifies it. (The secret is to choose the object immediately after a black object has been pointed out.) When another member of the group thinks he or she knows the secret, he or she tries being the cohort who guesses the object.

FAMOUS NUMBERS

Not only do people become celebrities, but sometimes particular numbers get added to the great "Number Hall of Fame," wherever that exists. Here are some famous numbers. Can you identify them?

Do you have a lucky number? Can you attribute any specific luck to your number? Would you care to share with the group why this is your lucky number? Do you recall your house number? Your phone number? Your zip code? Your area code?

We sure have become a society of numbers, haven't we?

1. Little Pigs:
     4   3   2
2. Baker's Dozen:
     11   12   13
3. Length of a football field:
     100 yards   100 feet   144 yards
4. Number of years that Rip Van Winkle slept:
     3   100   20
5. Winning hand in Blackjack:
     21   100   12
6. Dwarfs with Snow White:
     7   3   12
7. Santa's Reindeer:
     6 + Rudolph   8 + Rudolph   12 + Rudolph
8. Year of the Stock Market Crash:
     1914   1933   1929
9. Year of the Gold Rush:
     1849   1856   1776
10. Number of States in the United States:
     48   50   52
11. Number of days of Christmas:
     25   31   12
12. Letters in the English alphabet:
     21   26   36
13. Jack Benny's claimed age:
     21   57   39
14. Number of bones in the human body:
     121   206   309
15. Freezing point of a Fahrenheit scale:
     32 degrees   0 degrees   100 degrees
16. Number of players on a cricket, soccer, or football team:
     11   7   3
17. Number of legs on an octopus:
     6   8   12
18. James Bond's number:
     099   007   714

Continued

19. Number of years Sleeping Beauty slept:
    20   99   100
20. President Kennedy's P.T. boat number:
    P.T. 109   P.T. 45   P.T. 108
21. Prime Minister of England's address on Downing Street:
    10   13   26
22. Number of teeth the average person should have:
    64   28   32
23. The Day of Infamy:
    January 1, 1933   December 7, 1941   July 4, 1776
24. Famous Dice Numbers:
    7-11   3-6   2-4

ANSWERS

1. 3
2. 13
3. 100 yards
4. 20 years
5. 21
6. 7
7. 8 + Rudolph
8. 1929
9. 1849
10. 50
11. 12
12. 26
13. 39
14. 206
15. 32 degrees
16. 11
17. 8
18. 007
19. 100 years
20. P.T. 109
21. 10
22. 32
23. December 7, 1941
24. 7-11

OCCUPATIONS

There are no right or wrong answers to this challenge. Just stretch your imagination. The leader names an object and asks what occupations come to mind. The occupations can be directly or indirectly related to the object. For the sake of conversation, consider the objects listed.

1.	Pencil	16.	Microphone
2.	Shovel	17.	Television
3.	Typewriter	18.	Cash register
4.	Saw	19.	Potato
5.	Airplane	20.	Whiskey
6.	Microscope	21.	Gasoline
7.	Knife	22.	Tractor
8.	Stove	23.	Baseball
9.	Gun	24.	Clouds
10.	Stethoscope	25.	Animals
11.	Apron	26.	Rocks/stones
12.	Chalk	27.	Broom
13.	Book	28.	Piano
14.	Scale	29.	Patient
15.	Tire	30.	Glass

For example:
Occupations that come to mind because of a pencil are: An accountant, a school child, a draftsman, etc. Other occupations that are in existence and rely upon a pencil are: salesman (sells the pencils).

WHATZIT?

Instructions: Each box denotes a word, phrase, or saying. What does each box say or mean? (Answers on next page.)

SAND	MAN / BOARD	STAND / I	R E A D I N G
WEAR / LONG	R ROAD A D	T O W N	CYCLE CYCLE CYCLE
LE VEL	O / M.D. Ph.D. B.S.	KNEE / LIGHTS	II / OOO OO
CHAIR	DICE DICE	T O U C H	GROUND / FEET FEET FEET FEET FEET FEET
MIND / MATTER	HE'S/HIMSELF	ECNALG	DEATH/LIFE
G.I. / C C C C C C C	___ PROGRAM	B L O U S E	J U YOUSME T

Answers to Whatzit?

Sandbox	Man overboard	I understand	Reading between the lines
Long underwear	Crossroads	Downtown	Tricycle
Bilevel Split level	3 degrees below zero	Neon lights	Circles under the eyes
High chair	Paradise	Touchdown	6 feet underground
Mind over matter	He's beside himself	Backwards	Life after death
G.I. overseas	Space program	See-through blouse	Just between you and me

Speakers, Special Events, Outings

Speakers

The speakers selected for therapeutic recreation programs are not the same as those used during group counseling. TR speakers are used as resources for facilities, activities, and contacts in the community. Examples are:

- staff person from city parks and recreation department
- local photographer/camera shop owner
- arts and crafts store owner
- Radio Shack salesperson to discuss latest in VCR, tapedecks, CD players, etc.
- director from youth recreation club
- director and some members from local youth drama group
- leader from youth outdoor club
- bicycle store owner - to describe different types of bikes, uses, etc.
- leader from youth outdoor club or Sierra Club members
- travel agent or tour guide
- hobby enthusiast
- local celebrity

Special Events

- barbershop quartet
- Sweet Adelines
- community players
- parades
- caricature drawings
- Soberlympics

Outings

- zoo
- baseball, football, basketball, soccer games
- New Games Day
- rollerskating
- swimming
- local nursery and flower store
- the mall
- local restaurants

Chapter Ten
LEISURE SKILLS AND INTERESTS

Expressing a satisfying leisure lifestyle implies that an individual has a sense of freedom and choice in leisure involvement. Choices involve having options and alternatives.

It is important to acquire a broad variety of leisure skills, but more important to select and develop adequate skills in a number of activities that will be a potential source of enjoyment, satisfaction, and enrichment for the individual. McDowell (1983, p. 4) said, "People may not necessarily value so much what they are doing as recreation, but what they are feeling inwardly about doing it or having done it."

Skills and interests go hand-in-hand. Persons find activities that interest them and then develop the skills which enable them to participate in the activity. If they do not continue to develop and increase their skills in that activity, they will lose interest. A goal in TR is to expose the clients to a variety of activities to stimulate an interest. It is obvious that with the lack of time in an inpatient program, skills cannot be developed, but a client could get the basic concepts and continue learning new skills while in outpatient and community programs.

These activities will take place in a variety of settings through an organized delivery system, such as a bowling league, ceramics class, softball league, or photography club. Many activities will be done through commercial businesses, such as going to a show, dancing, visiting a health spa, attending a concert. Other activities will be done at home or in a variety of social environments with others.

Most CD persons are not motivated to develop skills, and they are void of interests. They do not have any ideas or the desire to do anything. It is a definite challenge to motivate these persons to develop skills and new interests.

A good way to start is to question the clients on hobbies they may have had as children. If they did have a hobby, it may be possible to rekindle that interest. Bring in guest speakers with a variety of interests and skills. Team and individual sports/games might be introduced. Always use lead-up games for these sports so the person can have small successes occurring at very short intervals. Physical fitness activities need to be introduced. Weight training and low impact aerobics seem to be popular with these persons. Walking, jogging, swimming, and bicycling are "in vogue" now and have appeal for this population.

There are many pencil and paper games to determine skills and interests. Some examples will appear in the leisure awareness portion of Chapter Eight in this book. Other leisure skills and interests are included in the communication/socialization activities (Chapter Nine) and family activities (Chapter Twenty-Six).

Chapter Eleven
RESOURCES

Awareness, identity, and utilization of leisure resources is an essential factor in developing a positive leisure lifestyle. Resources are within the individual, the family/home, peers, and the community. Resources involve people, activities, supplies and equipment, and facilities. Another important resource for CD persons is support groups.

Support groups are essential for CD persons. Every individual needs a person or people who will give support in one of four ways: emotional/comfort, appraisal/confrontal, informational/educational, and companionship. Seldom does one person give support in all four areas, nor is that a particularly good idea. Persons should have different support groups for different needs. AA/NA are major support groups. Mentors certainly fall in the support category. Peers, family, and community persons usually give support in one or more of the support areas. It is important that the CD person develop strong support systems in all four areas.

Self-support involves supporting yourself as well as supporting others. Do you like yourself? Are you comfortable being alone, or do you always need to be around others? Do you create, daydream, read, go for a walk, discover figures in the clouds? What are your skills and competencies? Think positive! What are the good things about YOU?

Family/Home. Leisure and recreational activities are done more at home than in any other place. There are many opportunities to interact and do things together. However, the CD family is often dysfunctional and may not be a support group. It might be that one person in the family is supportive and encouragement will come from this person. What types of things does your family do together? Do you joke, talk at meals, go shopping together, picnic, or travel? Do you share happenings, good and bad? Who taught you the recreational skills you now have? Do you have common recreational interests with other family members?

Family will be discussed more fully in Chapter Twenty-Six, Family Activities.

Peers are so important to all of us. What kinds of people do you choose to be around? Are you all the same? Do you argue? (What a dull world if we always agreed.) Do you have a variety of friends and do different things with different friends?

Think of someone who makes you laugh. Who is it? Why does this person make you laugh? We all need humor in our lives. Select people to be around who give you enrichment and positive strokes.

Community. How do you find resources in your community? What are you looking to do? Do your needs require people, a facility, or both? Where are the different recreational places? Where are places to meet new people?

It is important to make a list of things you want to do and then follow up. Make definite plans — where, when, with whom, how much does it cost? Each community is unique and offers a variety of activities and experiences.

Community resources include:

- City recreation department
- YMCA and YWCA
- YWHA and YWMA
- University or college programs
- Church programs
- School programs
- 4-H clubs, Boys' Clubs or Girls' Clubs
- Parents Without Partners clubs
- Women's clubs, men's clubs, senior citizen clubs
- City Chamber of Commerce can help locate facilities
- Scouting programs
- Local theatre groups
- Local library
- Weight Watchers
- Alcoholics Anonymous
- Narcotics Anonymous
- Welcoming organizations (Welcome Wagon)
- Arts and crafts shops and hobby shops
- Dance studios
- Museums and art galleries
- Local newspapers
- Community concert association
- Volunteer service organizations
- Bookstores
- Garden clubs
- Yellow pages of the telephone book
- Health spas
- Theaters
- Swimming pools
- Bowling alleys
- Tennis courts
- Malls
- Parks
- Zoos
- Outdoor areas for fishing, hunting, and skiing
- Scenic drives
- Nature trails
- Special interest shows (dog, flower, auto, circus)
- Playing fields
- Specialty shops
- Garage sales

SUPPORT GROUPS

We all need people to support us in some way. The following support systems (groups) can help an individual in different ways. Put the name of one or more persons in each of the squares below who help you in the way described on the left. You may use the same person in more than one box, but it is always wise to have a network of supports. Try to have at least three names in each box.

SUPPORT GROUP	PERSONAL	PROFESSIONAL
Emotional/Comforter Persons with whom you are willing to share your feelings, emotions, and reactions.		
Appraisal/Confrontal Someone who gives you honest opinions and constructive criticism. Helps you see alternatives. Often asks you questions you have avoided asking yourself.		
Informational/Educational Someone who gives information that aids in making decisions; gives educational-type information. Resources within the community.		
Companionship Persons with whom to go places and do things. Someone with whom you can have feelings of sharing and camaraderie.		

NO ONE is an

"I$_s$-LAND"

- One valuable "SURVIVAL SKILL" is having supports in our lives to help us cope.

- Fill in the names of your "SUPPORTS" above.

- If you were not able to fill in all 5, how or where can you find them?

_____
_____
_____
_____
_____

Source: © 1989, *Life Management Skills*. Reproducible activity handouts created for facilitators. Available from Wellness Reproductions, Inc. 1-800-669-9208.

BALANCE FORM

Instructions: List as many things to do as you can in each of the following areas:

Alone: With Spouse: With Friends: With Family:

_____   _____   _____   _____

_____   _____   _____   _____

_____   _____   _____   _____

_____   _____   _____   _____

Calm/Relaxing: Quiet: Noisy: Exhilarating/Active:

_____   _____   _____   _____

_____   _____   _____   _____

_____   _____   _____   _____

_____   _____   _____   _____

Spiritual: Self-Improvement: Creative: Just Plain Fun:

_____   _____   _____   _____

_____   _____   _____   _____

_____   _____   _____   _____

_____   _____   _____   _____

That Change the Scenery: That Stay at Home:

_____   _____

_____   _____

_____   _____

_____   _____

LEISURE FACILITIES POKER RUN

Participants are each given a large manila folder with their names on it. They're then taken to several leisure facilities and information centers (skating rink, campground, golf course, chamber of commerce, parks and recreation department, parks, community center, theaters, bowling alley, sporting goods store, museum, community swimming pool, library, nature center) and at each place staff are prepared to give them a playing card in a sealed envelope, along with any printed material they have available about what they offer.

When everyone is back at the treatment center, they open their envelopes and try to come up with their best possible poker hand. Prizes are certificates and merchandise from the places they visited. Best hand gets first choice, second gets second choice, etc. Have enough prizes so that each participant will receive one.

COMMUNITY RESOURCES AND PERSONAL FEELINGS

Category: Resources
Supplies: Brochures, flyers, newspapers
Age Level: Adolescent, adult
Time: 30 minutes
Objectives: To recognize activities that would alleviate "problem times"
                    To develop lists of resources for "problem" times
Description/Instructions: Collect brochures, flyers, and daily newspapers from local community. Have enough materials for each person if group is small or for each group of three if there are more than six people in the goupr.

Assign each person or each group a span of time (preferably two or three hours, although this may vary with the type of mood assigned) and specify day and a mood (happy, sad, frustrated, anxious, energetic, tired, etc.). Have persons find several activities that would meet their needs and/or alleviate the asssigned feeling.
Example: Person A is assigned: 1:00-3:00, Sunday afternoon, anxious. What can person A do during this time to make him or her feel better? Answer: symphony concert at Pershing Auditorium (relax and soothe the nerves); fun run at Pioneer Park (clear the mind); watch Little Guy football at elementary school (release tension.

WARM FUZZIES

All people like to hear positive things about themselves. Often they hear only negative things. Not only is it good to hear positive things about ourselves, but it is enjoyable to give compliments to others. All of us need to practice giving and receiving compliments. Too often CD persons have such low self-esteem that they cannot accept compliments; they simply do not believe them.

These positive things, or compliments, are called "warm fuzzies." People should give warm fuzzies every day. Hopefully, they will receive warm fuzzies every day.

People need to learn the skills of giving compliments. They should observe others and pick out the positive things about these other people. It takes very little effort to say, "Gee, I'm glad to see you today" or "You sure are good at cards" or "You have a great sense of humor." It is these little things that count and "make a person's day." In the TR programs, the staff should give warm fuzzies (role modeling) and constantly remind persons to give compliments. Also, staff can ask, "Who has received a warm fuzzie today? Who has given a warm fuzzie today?"

Chapter Twelve
ARTS AND CRAFTS

Arts and crafts make up one of our most challenging and satisfying recreational activities. There are many books dealing with this subject; therefore, this chapter lists only a few different types of arts and crafts and presents several specific activities.

Objectives: To develop new leisure interests.
To promote personal leisure enjoyment
To build self-esteem.
To express creativity.

Types

Tie dyeing
Sponge painting
Hand puppets
Homemade games
"Friendly" rocks
Painting
Clay work
Decoupage
Leatherwork
Origami
Wood sculptures
Jewelry making
Weaving
Macrame
Paper mache
Collage
Knitting/crocheting/embroidery
Mobiles

Stained glass:

Use napkins (fancy party napkins)
Take the design and cut it out - use only the top layer
Use white glue and glue the design to a jar
Cover with glitter if desired

Collages:

Use magazines, old cards, newspapers, and construction paper to make a collage

Potato Printing:

Cut potatoes in half
Distribute a half of a potato to everyone
Using forks, knives, toothpicks, etc. cut out or carve a design into the cut part of the
    potato
Using poster paints, dip the potato in the desired color and stamp onto white paper
Try exchanging the carved potato halves

Copper Tooling:

Cut piece of copper
Tape design to copper and trace
Turn copper over and start to push out the desired parts when finished, tack to a piece
    of board

Painting:

Use a piece of paper and some poster paint and express self through drawing
As a group create a mural — using large paper roll (tape on wall)

Tie Dye:

Dye a white shirt or whatever is available
Tie or knot the shirt
Dip in desired colors
Rinse in cold salt water to set

Ceramics:

Paint premolded ceramic statues

Fabric Painting:

Choose a design
Trace onto shirt
Paint using fabric designed paints
Allow to dry for a few hours

LEISURE BOX

Category: Arts and crafts
Supplies: Shoe box, beans, rice, noodles, other odds and ends, glue
Time: 30 minutes
Objectives: To provide social interaction
To promote awareness of leisure activities among groups of two or three people

Description/Instructions: Divide the participants into groups of two or three people. Each individual group decides on a leisure activity which they will make in the box. The groups make their scenes in their box with beans, rice, noodles, and any other odds and ends. After each group has made a leisure scene, they go around the room and look at the other boxes and guess what the scene is. Then each group talks about the leisure scene in their box.

Modifications: Use cardboard instead of boxes. Can also use construction paper. The class can do individual boxes or can be divided into larger groups.

Processing: Did the group come up with activities common among them?
Did you like working in small groups?
When you looked at and heard about the other groups' activities, did you learn any new leisure activities?
Were you pleased with your creation?

LEISURE EXPERIENCE

Category: Arts and crafts
Supplies: Large sheets of construction paper, variety of colors, one for each group; 8 x 11 construction paper, various colors, one for each person; glue, no scissors
Age Level: Adolescent, adult
Time: 30 minutes
Objectives: To be creative
To cooperate with group
To recall good experiences in leisure

Description/Instructions: Divide into groups of three to five persons. Each person selects one construction sheet, trying to get a variety of colors within the group. Each group selects one large sheet of construction paper.

Each group is to decide on a leisure experience that can be illustrated with construction paper. Groups are allowed 15 minutes in which to create. Then a spokesperson from each group will hold up the "creation" and explain it. Comments of praise are welcome from other groups.

May want to put these on display.

Chapter Thirteen
DANCE

Dance is "body expression." People hear music and automatically start expressing through body movement. Dance is probably one of the most personal and joyous forms of creative expression. It is a universal human phenomenon that has occurred in all ages and all cultures.

Dance should be part of all CD programs, inpatient, outpatient, and community. Programs should include social dances, instructional dance, and/or "fun" dances (those dances incorporated with other activities and which could include circle dances, singing dances, and fad dances). Let participants decide what type of dances they want to include for the social dances. They may want to bring their own tapes.

Dance categories include:

Modern, creative

Tap

Clogging

Square dance

Contras (Virginia Reel, Petronella)

Folk (polka, schottische)

International folk

Social ("mod," waltz, foxtrot, jitterbug, samba,
    rhumba, cha cha)

Circle/round (mixers)

Line or solo dances (Amos Moses, Hustle, The Pookie, Popcorn,
    Chicken)

Singing, also called play party games (Bingo, Skip to My Lou)

A reliable source for all kinds of records, with dance instructions, is Bob Ruff, 8459 Edmaru Ave., Whittier, CA 90605 (213) 693-5976. Several books containing dance instructions, with notes about available music, are available from the American Alliance for Health, Physical Education, Recreation and Dance, 1900 Association Drive, Reston, VA 22091 (1-800-321-0789).

Chapter Fourteen
CREATIVE EXPRESSION/DRAMA

Every person possesses some type of creativity. Creative activity immerses us fully in the here and now, and at the same time, it frees us. We become one with the activity and are nourished by it. This list notes some different ways to express creativity:

Cook/bake -- gourmet foods

Plan a party

Create a new game

Design a patio area

Make up different words to songs

Redecorate a room

Participate in performing arts (music, dance, drama)

Work with metals, wood, natural materials

Write clever invitations/letters

Write a poem or story

Play games such as Pictionary

Drama is one of the strongest forces in recreation to offer multiple opportunities to whet our thirst for creativity. It makes life more intense and meaningful and, besides, it is fun. Drama is the frosting on the cake. All of us enjoy "stepping out of ourselves." Drama opens doors, extends horizons, and sets the imagination free.

Charades are a type of drama that can be played many ways. Select the appropriate rules, explain the roles, and let the groups begin.

Several activities that help CD persons express creativity in different ways are presented in this chapter.

WHAT DO YOU SEE?

<u>Instructions:</u> Each person cuts out 10 pictures from different magazines on anything that appeals and suggests leisure to that person. Create a different and innovative caption for each picture. Share these captions with others. Might display on the wall for one or two days.

PHOTO IMAGERY

Instructions: An individual, several persons, or a family could put together a creative slide show that would express the new beginning or recovery of an independent lifestyle.

The group could choose a theme that would depict this "new beginning" and take pictures of nature, life, abstract objects, the family doing things together, or whatever it takes to help get across the idea of beginning again.

This could be set to music to add another dimension of mood and expression.

RECORD ALBUM COVER

Category: Creative Expression
Supplies: Art paper (14 x14 size), drawing materials (crayons, markers, pens, etc.), tables and chairs
Age Level: Adolescent
Time: 50 minutes
Objectives: To explore self-concept
              To creatively express
              To self-disclose in group to peers.

Description/Instructions: Each participant will create an album cover that illustrates self. Hand out paper and drawing materials to each participant. Ask the participants to think of themselves as a record and design an album cover. The album cover should illustrate self. It can be abstract or realistic. Also, on the back of the cover, list song titles that represent feelings.

Variations: Draw favorite "record album cover" and explain why it is your favorite.

Processing: Have each group member share their album cover and song titles.

CINQUAIN

Category: Creative Expression
Supplies: Examples of cinquains, pencil and paper
Age Level: Adolescent, adult
Time: 30 - 50 minutes
Objectives: To express creativity
              To become aware of surroundings

Description/Instructions: This activity is particularly effective when conducted in the outdoors. Each person sits apart from others. Describe anything that comes to mind:

Line 1 - Noun

Line 2 - Two adjectives that describe the noun

Line 3 - Three verbs that tell what the noun does

Line 4 - A phrase that tells something about the noun

Line 5 - The noun again, or a synonym, or a related word

Examples:

Tree,
Tall, brown
Swaying, creaking, growing
Leaves fluttering down
Oak

Dreams,
Happy, sad
Create, scare, soothe
Take you many different places
Dreams

Relaxation,
Gentle, soothing
Glides, rolls, flows
Releases energy
Relaxation

Swimming,
Active, refreshing
Float, stroke, glide
Movement in a supportive environment
Freestyle

THE MACHINE

Category: Creative Expression
Supplies: Machine component cards, machine-like music
Age Level: Adolescent, adult
Time: 30 - 45 minutes
Objectives: To creatively express oneself through play acting
                To practice cooperation within a group
                To become the center of group attention

Description/Instructions: Leader explains to players while handing out cards that each person is a component of a machine. Ask each player to imagine what the function of the part named on their card might be. Ask them to imagine how it might move.

Tell players to form a circle. The first component will be called out. That component must move to the center of the circle and move as that part might move.

When the next player's component is called, he or she must move to the center along with the other before him or her. He or she must build on the previous player's movement with his or her own, closely coordinating his or her machine-like movement with the person just before.

This continues until the machine has been assembled, all players (components) moving cooperatively. The leader now makes a motion to turn off the machine. Machine movements slow down and gradually the machine freezes.

The leader disassembles the machine.

Variation: Machine can function to the beats of different types of music.

Possible Component Names: divided bracket, turning spring, jolt lever, starter wheel, 2:1 gear, punch arm, cutter, piston, timing belt, finishing blade, rotating gismo, locating fixture, driving spindle, revolving watchamacallit, production belt, alternating thingamajig.

A DAY IN THE LIFE OF ...

Category: Drama
Supplies: Colored yarn, felt, glue, scissors, 12' rope, two bed sheets, tape, socks (white, brown, black), paper, pencils
Age Level: Adolescent
Time: Three days, 60 minutes each day
Objectives: Enhance self-expression skills
                Develop a further understanding of communication skills
                Develop creativity through crafts and drama

Description/Instructions:

Day One: Each participant is asked to choose a sock and make a puppet representing himself or herself. Yarn, felt, glue, and scissors are distributed to all participants.

113

Day Two: The participants are broken into groups of three or four. They are to write up one 12 minute script/play that centers around a feeling. These scripts can be either humorous or serious in nature, and the participants need to include:

(1) how they handle the feeling, and

(2) when does such a feeling occur.

As an option, the participant groups can choose a feeling to express or the activity leader can appoint them a feeling.

Day Three: The stage is constructed by stringing the rope across the room and attaching it so that it is at least four feet off the ground. The bed sheets are then hung over the rope so that the clients can hide behind them while holding the puppets above the sheet. The plays are then acted out.

Processing:

When all of the plays have been completed, each group identifies the feeling that they expressed, the reason it was chosen, or benefits derived from doing a play on it. Once this is completed, the activity leader should discuss the results when people fail to express their feelings such as: losing control of their temper, isolating, internal conflicts, creation of stress, depression, usage of alcohol, etc.

The group can also process what has happened to them personally when they didn't express their feelings. The positive aspects that can come from self-expression should be highlighted such as: opened communication, resolved problems. stress reduction, etc.

The leader can conclude the activity by stating that puppetry is only one of the many ways in which people can express their feelings.

HUMOR DRAMA EXERCISE

Instructions: Use the following situations or design other situations and distribute them to the group.

Group 1: Create a pantomime representing an everyday event involving a misunderstanding that results in much confusion and frustration.

Act out in pantomime: Mother picked up children from school. A few minutes later, father arrives thinking he is supposed to pick up the children, but they aren't there. Father finds out though a phone call that the family is at home waiting for him.

Group 2: Portray a TV commercial advertising a funny product or for a serious product using a humorous approach (cannot use hands or arms, but can speak).

Act out any given popular soap commercial, using humorous approach.

Group 3: Create a portrayal of primitive humans discovering a modern object such as a tape player, recreation equipment, or household objects. Use only nonsense sound and words to communicate.

114

Group 4: Develop a dramatization of a group of individuals in a recreational activity involving role reversal or out of the ordinary circumstances (attempting to lose, underwater checkers, taking on other's traits, etc.). Use all means of communication.

Processing: Which was easier to understand when different means
                   of communication were used?
               Is it difficult to get a message across when you don't have certain means of
                   communication?
               When you remove some of the communication means, the message may
                   become distorted.

Chapter Fifteen
MUSIC

Music is one of the greatest universal languages. A person can whistle, hum, sing, tap his or her fingers or feet to the beat, play an instrument, or dance to the rhythm. Music can be played on radio, tapes, television, compact discs, or an instrument. Without music our lives would not be complete. Music takes place anywhere, indoors, outdoors, any surface, and no experience is needed. It is enjoyable, unifies and equalizes people, and gives the opportunity for self-expression.

Music offers excellent opportunities for CD persons. It is "known" and therefore is not a threat. It offers great variety of choice, promotes and intensifies positive feelings, gives permission to move, allows each individual to respond in terms of his or her own skills and experiences, and can influence physical, psychological, and sociological behavior.

Types of music experience include:

1. Singing Groups

    A capella choirs, choruses, informal community sings, glee clubs, singing games

2. Instrumental Groups

    Rhythm bands, marching bands, chamber music groups, groups making and playing homemade instruments, special instrumental groups (banjo, guitar, etc.), symphony orchestras

3. Special Events

    Band concerts, pageants, musical festivals, old fiddlers contests, square dance caller contests, operas, original song contests

4. Cultural Groups

    Music appreciation clubs, study groups, musical composition

5. Songs

    Action, folk, hymns and carols, popular, round, spiritual, patriotic, songs of sentiment

6. Dance

    Rhythms, folk, square, social, fad

Every week during music session, some time can be spent on a featured variety of music. Examples are country, rock, gospel, classical, Indian, Big Bands, jazz, blues, and pop. Some songs will be played and discussed and tapes made available for those interested to check out from the group leader. Following are some ideas and specific activities for group music experiences.

My Favorite Song

Have everyone present their favorite song (on tape) and tell why they chose it and what the words say to them. Have other group members comment on what they think about the song. This will let people get to know each other without having to ask personal questions and it will also let other people learn about some new music.

Broadcasting, 1, 2, 3

Split the group up and give them a tape recorder and a tape. Have them record their favorite songs, do a newscast, present a commercial, and create a feature on leisure. After they get their broadcast recorded, have the groups play them for the others.

Matching

Have one person run the record player and the rest of the group is split into pairs. The leader begins playing the music and calls out instructions as to how the partners must face each other. For example, "face to face," "side to side," "back to back," "right hand to left hand." The leader then calls out, "change partners," trying to get a new partner, and the person left without a partner is the new leader. This game enhances personal trust and concentration.

Jingles

Split the group into small groups. Give them a piece of paper and a pencil. For five minutes let them brainstorm and write down names of jingles for commercials. After the five minutes are up, point to each group and have them sing one of the jingles, then point to the next group and have them sing one of theirs. Go around and around the groups until a group runs out of ideas. That group sits out and listens to the others. The groups cannot use the same jingles that another group has used. This will enhance cooperation and socialization.

Musical Costumes

Here is a funny game that allows everyone to look a little silly. Before you start, prepare a laundry bag or pillow case filled with various articles of clothing— funny hats, baggy pants, gloves, belts, or anything that can be worn. (The leader can use his/her own discretion as to how embarrassing the items are.) Keep the bag tied shut, so the clothing will not spill out.

Have your group form a circle and start passing the bag around as music is played. (If you don't use music, use some other random signal like an egg timer or automatic toaster to stop the action.) When the music stops, the person holding the bag must reach in and take out an article without looking. Then he or she must put it on and wear it for the remainder of the game. Try to have enough so each person gets three or four funny articles of clothing. Afterwards, one can have a fashion show or take pictures and hang them up.

Taken from the book *Play It: Great Games for Groups* by Wayne Rice and Mike Yaconelli, © 1986 by Youth Specialties, Inc. Used by permission of Zondervan Publishing House.

Guessing Songs

Players individually pantomime the act of singing a certain type of song. They do everything they can to express silently the nature and the mood of the song. The type of song may be announced beforehand to the viewers, or they may try to guess it. Suggestions include: patriotic songs, love songs, Indian songs, sad songs, cowboy songs, operatic songs, comic songs, sea shanties, lullabies, Christmas carols, military songs, sacred songs, Hawaiian songs, winter songs, Spanish songs.

What's in a Picture

Place pictures of all kinds (kids playing with a kite, a flower, a Christmas tree, the ocean, an eagle, a bulldog, a tennis shoe, heavy traffic, a mountain scene, friends, etc.) on one wall. Persons put a title or a line from a song on sheet below each picture, or have persons bring in music that they feel says something about the picture. Play the music and ask people to comment on how it relates to picture for them.

Lip Sync

Person or groups of people select a song and "lip sync."

Musical Bingo

Put names of songs on a bingo card. Play 30 seconds of different songs and have people block them out if they are on their bingo card. Must fill one line of five or could "black out" entire card.

EXPLORATIONS IN MUSIC

Category: Music
Supplies: Tape recorder, chairs in circle, extension cord
Age Level: Adolescent, adult
Time: 50 minutes
Objective: To enhance self expression skills and to give an opportunity to share

Description/Instructions: Participants bring their favorite tape. A discussion takes place noting that only positive reactions will be allowed during the entire session. Stress the importance of respecting other persons' choices and reasons for those choices.

Each person plays two to three minutes of a song. He or she then tells why it is a favorite song. Answers such as "it just is" require encouragement so that the person can express a feeling, reflect on a mood, or recall a memory. Others also may add their thoughts and feelings for the song.

Processing: Discuss how music is important in everyone's life.

Music can be used to express or represent feelings for each individual.

Music influences through tempo, tone, and rhythm.

Music can be used to increase our understanding of our feelings, communicate our feelings, relieve stress, and build up energies, which are all positive aspects of self-expression.

118

MUSICAL NAMES

Category: Music/Social Recreation
Supplies: Pencils, copy of activity for each person
Age Level: Adults, older adults
Time: 45 - 50 minutes
Objectives: To recall songs
                To think of music in different ways
                To have fun with group and music

Description/Instructions: Divide into groups of three. Tell the group members to "put on their thinking caps and answer the following challenges":

Can you name at least 5 songs in each of the following categories?

1. Name of a flower in the title:

_____   _____   _____

_____   _____

2. A specific geographic location in the title:

_____   _____   _____

_____   _____

3. Name of a male in the title:

_____   _____   _____

_____   _____

4. Name of a female in the title:

_____   _____   _____

_____   _____

5. An animal is mentioned in the title:

_____   _____   _____

_____   _____

Continued

6. The word "heart" is mentioned in the title:

_____   _____   _____

_____   _____

7. A mode of transportation is mentioned in the title:

_____   _____   _____

_____   _____

8. A color is in the title:

_____   _____   _____

_____   _____

9. A number is in the title:

_____   _____   _____

_____   _____

10. The word "moon" is in the title:

_____   _____   _____

_____   _____

11. An occupation:

_____   _____   _____

_____   _____

12. A food item:

_____   _____   _____

_____   _____

Continued

MUSICAL NAMES, continued

13. A body of water:

_____   _____   _____

_____   _____

14. A season or specific time of the year:

_____   _____   _____

_____   _____

ANSWERS

Here are some suggested song titles as answers to the questions. This definitely is not a complete list, just a few to get you started.

FLOWERS:

Red Roses for a Blue Lady
Yellow Rose of Texas
My Wild Irish Rose

Rose of Picardy
Daisy
When You Wore a Tulip

LOCATION:

By the Sea
Red River Valley
Carry Me Back to Old Virginny
Down by the Old Mill Stream
Home on the Range
Down on the Farm
Tavern in the Town
I Left My Heart in San Francisco
Jersey Bounce
Comin' Round the Mountain

Moonlight in Vermont
America the Beautiful
Blue Hawaii
My Old Kentucky Home
Deep in the Heart of Texas
On Top of old Smokey
South of the Border
Meet Me in St. Louis
It's a Long Way to Tipperary
Sidewalks of New York

MALE:

Casey Jones
Old MacDonald Had a Farm
Mack the Knife
Alexander's Ragtime Band
John Brown's Body

When Johnny Comes Marching Home
Waiting for the Robert E. Lee
H-A-R-R-I-G-A-N
Michael, Row the Boat Ashore

Continued

MUSICAL NAMES, continued

FEMALE:

Rosie O'Grady

I Dream of Jeannie

My Darling Clementine

Ida

Sweet Adeline

Daisy

Mary

Goodnight Irene

Ramona

Peg o' My Heart

Mame

If You Knew Susie

ANIMALS:

Three Little Fishies

Rudolph the Red Nosed Reindeer

How Much Is That Doggie in the
Window

Bye, Bye, Blackbird

Blue Bird of Happiness

The Old Grey Mare

The Donkey Serenade

Turkey in the Straw

Alley Cat

HEART:

Peg o' My Heart

Heartaches

Deep in the Heart of Texas

I Left My Heart in San Francisco

Dear Hearts and Gentle People

You Belong to My Heart

Heart of My Heart

TRANSPORTATION:

Sailing, Sailing

In My Merry Oldsmobile

Bicycle Built for Two

Red Sails in the Sunset

Cruising Down the River

Anchors Aweigh

Caissons Go Rolling Along

Fly Me to the Moon

Row, Row, Row Your Boat

I'm Leaving on a Jet Plane

COLOR:

Blue Hawaii

Red Roses

Yellow Rose of Texas

By the Light of the Silvery Moon

Silver Threads Among the Gold

Lavender Blue

My Blue Heaven

Deep Purple

Put on Your Old Grey Bonnet

NUMBERS:

Four Leaf Clover

Three Blind Mice

Twelve Days of Christmas

We Three Kings of Orient Are

Tea for Two

Five Foot Two

Sixteen Tons

Three Fishermen

Continued

MUSICAL NAMES, continued

MOON:

Shine On, Harvest Moon
Moonlight in Vermont
Moon Over Miami
By the Light of the Silvery Moon
Fly Me to the Moon
In the Evening by the Moonlight

Moon River
Carolina Moon
When the Moon Comes over the
    Mountain
On Moonlight Bay

OCCUPATIONS:

The Marine's Hymn
The Little Shoemaker
I've Been Working on the Railroad
The Man on the Flying Trapeze

Rosie the Riveter
McNamara's Band
Shrimp Boat Song
Banana Boat Song

FOOD and DRINKS:

In the Shade of the Old Apple
    Tree
Tangerine
Don't Sit Under the Apple Tree
Candy

Lemon Tree
Who Put the Overalls in Mrs.
    Murphy's Chowder
Rum and Coca Cola
Scotch and Soda

BODY OF WATER:

Blue Danube
Swanee River
Up a Lazy River
By the Sea

Down By the River Side
Erie Canal
Old Man River
My Bonnie Lies over the Ocean

SEASONS OR SPECIFIC TIME OF THE YEAR:

White Christmas
Autumn Leaves
In the Good Old Summertime
School Days
April Showers

Autumn in New York
April in Paris
In Your Easter Bonnet
Take Me Out to the Ball Game
Springtime in the Rockies

WHAT'S MISSING IN THE TITLE?

Fill in the missing words from the following song titles: How about singing the song?

1. Who Put the ... in Mrs. Murphy's ...?
2. My ... Irish ...
3. ... of my ...
4. I Left My ... in ...
5. On the ... in ... City
6. ... Sails in the ...
7. Five Foot ...
8. ... a ... Ribbon
9. In the ... of the Old ...
10. ... Me Out to the ...
11. I've Been ... on the ...
12. When ... and ... Were ..., Maggie
13. Every Little ... Seems to ... Louise
14. I'm Just ... About ...
15. ... of the Border, Down ... Way
16. O ... All Ye ...
17. Alexander's ... Band
18. The ... Went Over the ...
19. Don't Sit ... the ... Tree
20. ... Hearts and ... People
21. For ... a Jolly Good ...
22. By the ... of the .... Moon
23. God Bless ...
24. Bicycle ... for ...
25. Carry Me ... to Old ...
26. You Are My ...
27. Yes, Sir, That's My ...
28. ... the ... Nosed Reindeer
29. Nobody Knows the ... I've ...
30. Michael ... the ... Ashore
31. ... on the Flying ...
32. Let Me ... You ...
33. Give My ... to ...
34. How You Gonna Keep 'em ... on the ...
35. Cruising Down the ...
36. America the ...
37. For ... and ... Gal
38. Swing ... Sweet ...
39. When ... Comes ... Home
40. She'll Be ... Round the ...
41. I Want a ...
42. O, Little ... of ...
43. Meet Me in ... ...
44. Onward, ... Soldiers
45. O, What a ... We Have in ...
46. Shuffle Off to ...
47. Did Your ... Come From ...
48. It's a Long Way to ...
49. On the Road to ...
50. Sidewalks of ... ...
51. Way Down Yonder in ... ...
52. ... by the ... Stream
53. Deep in the ... of ...
54. Don't ... Me in
55. ... ... Is Coming to ...
56. I'm Dreaming of a ... ...
57. It Came Upon a ... Clear
58. You're a ... Old ...
59. ... Threads among the ...
60. When You Wore a ...
61. Somebody ... My Gal
62. Put Your ... Around Me ...
63. ... He's Making ... at Me
64. On ... of Old ...
65. ... a Grand Old Name
66. ... Goes the ...
67. ..., ... The Gang's All ...
68. Go ... It on the ...
69. I Dream of ...
70. I'll ... You in My ...
71. ... ... a Little Closer
72. The ... Played on
73. Ain't We Got ...
74. Is It ... What They Say about ...
75. Goodnight ...
76. How ... I Am
77. Ida, Sweet as ... ...
78. Let the ... of the ... Go By
79. Let a ... Be Your ...
80. Oh, My Darling ...
81. Put on Your Old ... ...
82. ... of Ages
83. Old ... Had a ...
84. Oh You Beautiful ...
85. The Old Grey ...
86. Now Is the ...
87. Pack Up Your ... in Your Old ... ...

Continued

124

88.   Shine on ... ...
89.   Waiting for the ... ...
90.   When I Grow Too ... to ...
91.   You Can't Be ... Dear
92.   There Is a ... in the ...
93.   In Your ... Bonnet
94.   Three Blind ...

95.   Show Me the ... to Go ...
96.   While Strolling Thru'
          the ... One ...
97.   Peg o' My ...
98.   Over ...
99.   My Old ... Home
100. Old ... at Home

ANSWERS TO WHAT'S MISSING

1. Overalls ... Chowder
2. Wild ... Rose
3. Heart ... Heart
4. Heart ... San Francisco
5. Boardwalk ...Atlantic
6. Red ... Sunset
7. Two
8. Tie ... Yellow
9. Shade ... Apple Tree
10. Take ... Ball Game
11. Working ... Railroad
12. You ... I ...Young
13. Breeze ... Whisper
14. Wild ... Harry
15. South ... Mexico
16. Come ... Faithful
17. Ragtime
18. Bear ... Mountain
19. Under ... Apple
20. Dear ... Gentle
21. He's ... Fellow
22. Light ... Silvery
23. America
24. Built ... Two
25. Back ... Virginny
26. Sunshine
27. Baby
28. Rudolph ... Red
29. Trouble ... Seen
30. Row ... Boat
31. Man ... Trapeze
32. Call ... Sweetheart
33. Regards ... Broadway
34. Down ... Farm

35. River
36. Beautiful
37. Me ... My
38. Low ... Chariot
39. Johnny ... Marching
40. Coming ... Mountain
41. Girl
42. Town ... Bethlehem
43. St. Louis
44. Christian
45. Friend ... Jesus
46. Buffalo
47. Mother ... Ireland
48. Tipperary
49. Mandalay
50. New York
51. New Orleans
52. Down ... Old Mill
53. Heart ... Texas
54. Fence
55. Santa Claus ... Town
56. White Christmas
57. Midnight
58. Grand ... Flag
59. Silver ... Gold
60. Tulip
61. Stole
62. Arms ... Honey
63. Ma ... Eyes
64. Top ... Smokey
65. Mary's
66. Pop ... Weasel
67. Hail ... Hail ... Here
68. Tell ... Mountain

Continued

69. Jeannie
70. See ... Dreams
71. Cuddle Up
72. Band
73. Fun
74. True ... Dixie
75. Irene
76. Dry
77. Apple Cider
78. Rest ... World
79. Smile ... Umbrella
80. Clementine
81. Grey Bonnet
82. Rock
83. MacDonald ... Farm
84. Doll

85. Mare
86. Hour
87. Troubles ... Kit Bag
88. Harvest Moon
89. Robert E. Lee
90. Old ... Dream
91. True
92. Tavern ... Town
93. Easter
94. Mice
95. Way ... Home
96. Park ... Day
97. Heart
98. There
99. Kentucky
100. Folks

Chapter Sixteen
TABLE GAMES/CARD GAMES

Table games and card games can be played individually, by people of all ages to share mental activities. The games can be cooperative and competitive. They offer socialization, fun and laughter, and opportunities to play familiar games and learn new ones to increase positive self esteem and to challenge oneself mentally.

Some types of table games or card games will be familiar for CD persons. Even if they have never played any of these games, most are easy to learn. These games are an excellent lifetime activity as well as giving opportunities as mentioned above.

Table games include:	Card games include:
The Ungame	Crazy Eights
Clue	Solitaire (different forms)
Checkers/Chess	Speed
Chinese Checkers	War
Backgammon	Go Fish
Monopoly	Old Maid
Parcheesi	Uno
Pictionary	Euchre
Scrabble	Thirteen
Boggle	Hearts
Yahtzee	Skipbo
Stratego	Slapjack
Battleship	Twenty One
Dominoes	I Doubt It
Encore	Pinochle
Outburst	Five Hundred
Trivial Pursuits	Card Tricks

You can also try creating your own games.

SEE IT - GOT IT

Category: Table Games
Supplies: 25 cent piece, hacky sack, 6" square piece of carpet or soft material on which to toss coin, long table, chair for each person
Age Level: Adolescent, adult
Time: 10 - 20 minutest
Objectives: Communication, competition, touch

Description/Instructions:
The client group is divided into two teams, each team sitting across from the other, with the table between them. The carpet piece is at the head of the table, where the leader stands. The hacky sack is placed on the table between the last two opponents. Each team holds hands. The two people who are at the head of the table, each on the opposite side, look at the leader who has the coin. The rest of the clients look down toward the opposite end of the table.

The leader then flips the coin onto the carpet piece. If it lands on "heads" the first two opponents then squeeze the hand of their teammates. This squeeze passes down until it reaches the last members who immediately try to grab the hacky sack. The first opponent to grab the hacky sack wins. That person's line then rotates up one seat, with the first person at the head of the table going to the last seat. The first team to fully rotate through and bring the original person back to the front wins.

If "tails" is thrown, no "squeezes" are passed. If "tails" is thrown and person grabs the hacky sack, that team loses one point.

Processing: Did you feel under pressure?
                 Did you feel like part of the group?
                 How did it feel to cooperate with others?
                 Was it fun?
Holly Guzman

SHIP, CAPTAIN, CREW

Category: Table Games
Supplies: A cup like that used in a Yahtzee game or in a Backgammon game, five dice
Age Level: Adolescent, adult
Time: 30 - 50 minutes
Objectives: To develop new recreational interests and skills

Description/Instructions: The object is to roll the dice and obtain a 6, a 5, and a 4 in a maximum of three rolls. The 6 must be obtained first, then the 5, and the 4 last. When each number is obtained that die is removed from play. The last two dice are used to score "the point" and are rolled to obtain the highest

Example: I roll the five dice and obtain the 6, 5, and 4 immediately and the last two dice are a 1 and a 3 for a score of 4. I have two throws left and elect to roll again this time obtaining a score of seven. With one throw left I roll again hoping to get a higher number this time obtaining a 12 or "boxcars" which is an automatic winner and a new game is to be started. If two players tie on the "point" then all players get to roll once more to try to obtain the highest point. Each person takes turns until one player wins.

GUGGENHEIM

Category: Table Games
Supplies: Paper and pencil
Age Level: Adolescent, adult
Time: 20 minutes
Objectives: To facilitate exposure and stimulate thinking in regard to leisure activities in a number of settings and situations

Description/Instructions: Papers are blocked off in squares with categories written in each of the squares across the top, eliminating the top left one. A word is chosen and written in the vertical squares, leaving the top one blank. The object of the game is to fill in the spaces using letters on the left as first letters for the categories at the top of the box. Be aware that words such as a, the, an, and, of, and in do not count as first words; also that in an answer of two words, the first letter of the first word is the one that counts, and in a proper name, the first letter of the last name.

It is best for your score if you can think of unusual answers. This is the way the scoring goes: if you have a correct answer and no one else has the same, you are given five points; if two people have it, three points; if three people have it, one point. If more than three people have it, there is no score. With a large group, you may have each individual add his or her own score, allowing one point for each acceptable answer.

Example Sheet:

	Dogs	Cities	Ice Cream Flavors	Cars	Candy bars
O					
P					
E					
N					

Processing: Was there a category you had trouble completing? Why?

In what way did you approach this game; were you anxious, or nervous with the time limit? Do you consider yourself a competitive person?

If you did experience anxiety, can you see how it may interfere with your thought processes?

Some people claim they work better under pressure; are you one? Why do you think you do?

LEISURE CONCENTRATION

Print pairs of cards with related leisure terms (an activity and a skill needed to do it, or the equipment involved, etc.). Beneath the printed activity, print the related word in parentheses. On the second card, print the related word with the activity under it in parentheses. Shuffle the cards and place one at a time face down on the table. Participants take turns turning up two cards. If the cards match, the participant keeps them. If not, they are turned face down on the table (in the same positions) and the next person takes a turn. If the participant does match the pair, he or she gets another turn besides keeping the cards. At the end of the game, the person with the most cards wins.

A good project is for the participants to make up a set of cards themselves. A good number with which to start would be five pairs. Gradually increase to 10 - 15 pairs of related cards.

Possible card pairs:

Concert - Michael Jackson   Visiting - Friends

Swimming - Bikini   Poetry - Cinquain

Horseback Riding - Saddle   Bridge - Cards

Camping - Sleeping Bag   Chinese Cooking - Wok

Drama - Charades   Canoe - Paddle

Baseball - Hotdog   Relaxation - Daydream

Chapter Seventeen
GAMES AND ACTIVITIES

Informal games, initiative games, trust activities, and adventure-based activities all interrelate. These four subdivisions of games will be introduced individually, followed by representative activities in each category. The author has tried the games presented here with CD populations. Some are appropriate with adolescents and some with adults, and some with either age level.

Informal Games

Informal games are those games that are done "just for the fun of it!" Usually they are brief, have few rules, do not require high levels of skill, and have great potential for social interaction and positive self-esteem.

The New Games concept encompasses having fun, with everyone a winner. The only rule is "play hard, play fair, nobody hurt." New Games are an excellent tool in developing positive self-esteem, fairness of play, cooperation, leadership, and awareness of different types of activities. New Games are mentioned as an excellent resource, although no activities are specifically described in this book (see list of references for titles of books containing New Games).

Finger Fencing

Face a partner. Hold your own left foot with own left hand. Grasp index finger of partner who is in same holding position. Object is to get partner off balance.

Handcuffs

Partners each have a two-foot string, which is tied loosely around both wrists. The two strings should loop through each other. The object is to separate intertwining string. Yes, it can be done!

Rope Map

The group has a long rope or piece of string. They make an outline of the United States with it, making it large enough so that they can all fit inside the borders. Then have them do the following:

1. Go to place where you were born. Name town and state.

2. Go to place where you had the best vacation. Tell us about it.

3. Go to place where you want to live. Why?

Kai Yi Yi Yi

Sit in circle with lower legs crossed and knees touching people on either side. Each person has a stone. Start kai yi chant as pass stone from own left hand to right hand and then pass to person on right ... at the same time receiving stone from person on left. Increase tempo of chant. Stop. Those persons having no stone or having more than one stone must sit in the middle. Remaining persons start chant and pass stones again. Repeat. However, don't make persons sit in the center more than three rounds of playing.

© 1991, A. Rainwater

Elbow Grab Tag

One person is the "chaser." Set area boundaries. Play by whatever tag rules you are used to, with the exception that you are safe only if you grasp elbows with another person. You cannot grasp elbows with same person consecutively or for more than ten seconds. When group is used to this, have them grasp by threes, then fours, or more.

Bocce (Boccie)

Regular set has four red balls, four green balls, and one smaller black ball (the jack). Can use croquet balls for the red and green balls and use golf ball for the jack.

Divide into teams of four each (two teams). One person rolls the jack. Everyone gets in a circle equidistant from the jack (same distance as person who rolled the jack). Same person who rolled the jack gets first turn. Opposite team then rolls. Object is to get closest to the jack. Then team having ball closest to jack gives other team the roll. Whichever team is furthest away continues to roll. When all balls have been thrown, the one closest gets one point. If two teams have balls equidistant, each team gets one point. Play to 21, or whatever score is determined before the game starts.

Gut Frisbee

Form two teams of any number. Designate outside boundaries of an area. Have a 20 foot neutral zone in the center of the playing area. Object of game is to throw the frisbee over the neutral zone into other team's area in such a manner that the frisbee cannot be caught with one hand. If team catches frisbee, it is thrown back across the neutral zone. If frisbee is dropped, the throwing team earns one point. Whichever side the frisbee is on (whether dropped or caught) throws the frisbee back to other side. If frisbee lands in neutral zone or out of bounds, the intended receiving team gets a point. Usually play to 21 points, but winning score can be determined before game starts.

Frisbee Golf

Set up a golf course, numbering the holes (areas or obstacles). Count frisbee throws same as would score for golf. Can play teams or individually.

132

Frisbee Horseshoes

Mount wire circle on peg which is driven into ground. Peg has 4' string for measuring distance. Same rules as horseshoes, but throw frisbee. Five points if frisbee goes through ring, two points for leaner, one point for team having frisbee closest to peg (within distance of end of string).

Frisbee Field Ball

First version: Two teams. One team spreads out over floor or field. Batting team member throws frisbee and immediately starts running around own team members (they should get in a line behind home plate). Runner must stop when field team raises frisbee over head of last person in their line. (Those in the field line up behind person who caught the frisbee and pass it over and under to last person who holds it up.) A total five batters (depends on number of persons on team). Add total number of runs around own team. Other team comes to bat and the procedure is repeated. Determine number of innings before starting the game.

Second version: Home plate and three bases placed in regular diamond shape. Batting team member throws frisbee. Entire batting team must run around the bases and touch home plate before last fielder in line can get the frisbee and run to marker by home plate. (As in the first version, the fielding team lines up behind teammate catching frisbee and must pass it over and under to last person in line.) If runner beats the fielder then one point is scored. If fielder beats any of team, then it is an "out." Three outs and other team comes to bat.

Sidewalk Tennis

Use tennis ball. Two people stand on sidewalk lines, two sidewalk blocks being used, and using the crack between as the net. Use rules of ping pong.

Balloon Basketball

Object: Score 10 points by getting balloon through the basket. Two points are scored per basket.

Instructions : Two teams are lined up opposite each other (4' apart) all lined up in chairs. Players must have hips on chair at all times. One person stands at each end and positions arms like a hoop. Referee tosses balloon into area between the lines and calls how the balloon must be hit: both hands, right hand, left hand, left foot, both feet, etc. Players from one line try to make basket at one end and at same time try to prevent other line from making basket at the other end.

Balloon Keep Up

Small groups join hands in a circle. Try to keep two or three balloons in the air. No hands. Add several more balloons.

Moon Ball

Scatter any size group across a basketball court or a field. Use a well inflated beach ball. Object of the game is to hit the ball aloft as many times as possible before the ball hits the ground. Set a goal of 30 - 100 hits to add incentive. Rules: A player cannot hit the ball twice in succession. Count one point for each hit and two points for a kick.

Adapted from: K. Rohnke. 1989. © Project Adventure,Inc.

The Wave, or Butt-Off

Sit in a circle with sturdy chairs fairly close together. One person is IT and leaves his or her chair and stands within the circle. As soon as the IT person moves toward an empty chair, that chair must be filled by the person sitting next to it, which will result in a clockwise movement of people. As one person moves, the next person must be in motion, in order to fill the rapidly vacating seat.

When the IT person finally gets his or her posterior into the appearing/disappearing empty chair, the displaced person must immediately look for and pursue the elusive empty chair. No timeouts. If someone becomes too exhausted to continue, let the IT person designate his or her own replacement. Change directions (from clockwise) occasionally to confuse and confound a floundering IT.

Adapted from: K. Rohnke. 1989. © Project Adventure, Inc.

Frisalevio

Object of the game is for one team to capture another group of equal size and place them in an outlined jail area. Equipment needed is ropes to outline jail area, approximately 10' x 10' and frisbees for half the players on one side.

Construct a jail in middle of a field. Give frisbees to one team (jailers) and have them stay inside the jail until word is given to GO. The potential inmates run anywhere in the field. Play begins as jailers attempt to capture inmates by throwing frisbees at them. If hit below the waist, the captured inmate must put both hands over his or her head and jog to jail. An uncaught inmate may at any time attempt to touch both feet inside jail area before being hit with a frisbee and shout FRISALEVIO in order to release all jailed inmates.

Rules: Frisbees may be thrown over and over by jailers. A frisbee may not be touched by an inmate. Reasonable boundaries need to be set. As soon as all potential inmates have been caught, change sides. If this takes too long, may set a time limit and count number of inmates at end of time period.

Adapted from: K. Rohnke. 1989. © Project Adventure,Inc.

134

Initiative Games

Initiative games continually put participants in situations where they must work as a group to solve problems. They are given a set of parameters and safety guidelines to a problem and are asked to solve the problem in the easiest and most efficient way. There is no right or wrong way, so persons have freedom to experiment.

Participants need to be involved with their bodies, mind, and emotions to be successful. Initiative games motivate persons to persist in solving a problem, which is an important aspect for CD populations. Anything that can motivate them is important.

Knots

To form knot, stand in a circle, shoulder to shoulder, and place your hands in the center. Everyone grabs hand of two different people. Do not grab two hands of one person, or the person next to you. Now unravel the knot, by using suggestions and moves by everyone until you are in a single circle. No one can release hands during the unraveling. Once in awhile you will get two circles. Amazing!

Plane Crash

Plane crashes high in the Himalayas and burns, blinding all of the people aboard. Two Sherpas come upon the scene and guide the people down the mountain and to safety. However, the Sherpas do not speak English, so must find another form of communication to guide the blind people to safety.

Two people are designated as the Sherpas. The other people all have blindfolds. Sherpas must decide how to communicate and then lead blind people through all types of obstacles (works best in the out of doors). Discuss the dependence and assistance that takes place. How did people feel?

Trust Activities

Trust is defined as the firm reliance on the integrity, ability, or character of a person or thing. The importance of trust development is well recognized. "Faith and trust in self and the other person is such an essential ingredient in relationships that it cuts across and interacts with all other components . . . of the self-concept system (Fitts, 1970, p. 15). Erikson's eight stages of human development and Maslow's "hierarchy of needs" identify trust as one of the most important basic needs of an individual. Schoel, Prouty, and Radcliffe (1988, p. 15) stated, "Without trust there is no 'glue' to hold relationships together, and indeed no identity possibility."

CD persons have abused the trust in them that others once had. This lack of trust is a consequence of their own actions, but also it is found that frequently they do not trust others or themselves. To build trust is a slow and delicate process.

Trust activities start with basic requirements of physical trust. Each person must prove that he/she is trustworthy in physical risk situations. When this has been accomplished, the psychological and social issues are introduced through activities. An example would involve taking physical risks *and* emotional risks (fear on a high ropes course) in which the full support from other participants allows a person to express fear, but also express pride and elation when the task has been completed.

Trust must be built and this takes time. There are a variety of activities that can be utilized to help foster the formation of trust; a few are presented here.

Self-Disclosure

Activities can include two persons or a small group. Be sure that all persons are willing to follow the rule: Respect everyone, regardless of whether you agree or disagree with what they are saying.
1. If you could be anything you wanted, what would it be?
2. Share a dream.
3. What was your most embarrassing moment?
4. What has been your scariest experience?
5. Tell us your favorite joke.
6. What is your most significant childhood memory?
7. What do you like most about your partner, spouse, or child (depending on what age level is involved)?

Trust Circle

(This game has many different names and is in many books.)
Participants stand shoulder to shoulder in a circle, arms in front of them, and feet in a bracing position. One person stands in the center of the circle, with arms folded across the chest, and keeps the body stiff. That person lets body fall against the hands of circle members, who push the person around and across the circle. After one person has been in the center for one minute, he or she exchanges places with another person from the circle.

Processing: How did you feel when you first leaned toward someone in the circle? Did you trust everyone? Did you have any fears? Was it difficult to keep your body stiff and your feet stationary? How did those of you in the circle feel? Did you want the center person to trust you? How did you convey this to that person? Did you want to try being the center person?

Individual Fall

Two persons stand one behind the other, both facing the same way, and about one foot apart. The front person crosses arms over chest, stands rigid, and gently falls backward into the hands (palms facing forward) of partner. Partner has braced self by keeping feet shoulder length apart and placing one foot forward and other back for strong balance. Front person then moves forward 6 inches and repeats falling backward into partner's hands. This distance increase is repeated until the receiving partner can no longer support the weight of falling person. Then exchange roles whereby the catching partner becomes the falling partner.

This activity can be used effectively in family activities. The mother or dad may have to get down on knees in order for child to catch him or her. Might also need a "spotter" to help the child. The larger person may also want to get on knees when catching a much smaller person.

136

Processing: Faller, did you trust your partner? Was it hard to fall backwards?
                      Faller, did you continue to trust partner as distance increased?
                      Receiver, were you confident you could catch partner?
                      Receiver, did you want partner to trust you?
                      Both, did this build trust in other person? How?

Blindfolded Trust Games

There are several activities in which one person is blindfolded and must trust another person to lead or "talk" him or her through a variety of obstacles.

1. Lead a blindfolded person all over an area. Then have that person try to find his or her way back to starting point. Sighted person walks behind and observes safety factors.

2. "Talk" a blindfolded person through an obstacle course. Be creative in this activity. Example: Person is Spaceship Sponzle. Person must maneuver around stars (other sighted persons spaced around an area) as well as stay away from Spaceships Zap and Zinger (other persons making appropriate noises and changing positions often).

You Be the Driver

The first step is to ask a person if they will be your partner. If the person refuses, ask another person, until you find someone who is willing to do this activity with you. (This is a good experience as forerunner to asking for a mentor when person has completed inpatient program.)

One person is the "car." He or she can select kind and color of car. (Make a big deal of this selection.) This person is blindfolded and must depend on the driver to get him or her to the designated place. Driver cannot touch the car, but gives instructions while going through many obstacles. Driver should be creative in giving instructions, e.g., "Move to the left lane and be ready to turn within 25 feet. Watch out for a bicycle rider who has just drawn up by your left rear wheel." Verbal instructions continue until destination is reached. This should take about 10 minutes. Then switch roles.

Processing: Car, did you feel helpless and dependent upon your driver?
                      Car, did you get good directions?
                      Car, as directions continued, did you gain confidence?
                      Driver, what did you do to make car trust you?
                      Driver, did you trust yourself in giving directions? It is important one build trust in others, but also behave in a manner that invites trust from others.

Adventure-Based Activities

Adventure-based activities can elicit a range of behaviors, feelings/emotions, and attitudes as well as challenge physically and mentally. They incorporate trust, challenge, cooperation, and excitement. They enable a person to test his/her physical and emotional limits. These things should be kept in mind when determining objectives and the activities to be used in meeting the objectives.

In *Islands of Healing: A Guide to Adventure-Based Counseling* (1990), Schoel, Prouty, and Radcliffe have devised objectives and sequencing (building from simple to complex skills, physically, mentally, and emotionally) in the following categories of adventure-based activities:

1. ice breaker/acquaintance
2. de-inhibitizer
3. trust and empathy
4. communication
5. decision making/problem solving
6. social responsibility
7. personal responsibility.

Objectives and features for each category are briefly described in this chapter. Activities in each category are listed under the book title in which the activity descriptions can be found.

This material is based on the book by Schoel, Prouty, and Radcliffe and used with the permission of the publisher, Project Adventure, Inc.

Ice Breaker/Acquaintance Activities

Objectives:

To provide opportunities for group members to get to know each other and to begin feeling comfortable with each other through activities, Initiatives and games that are primarily fun, nonthreatening and group-based.

Features:

Fun is a major component.
Group members interact in a nonthreatening manner.
Success-oriented; tasks can be easily accomplished with
   minimal amount of frustration.
Requires minimal verbal interaction and decision making skills.

De-Inhibitizer Activities

Objectives:

To provide a setting wherein group participants are able to take some risks as well as make improvement in commitment and a willingness to appear inept in front of others.

ICE BREAKER/ACQUAINTANCE ACTIVITIES

Cowstails and Cobras
Add on Tag
Aerobic Tag
Balance Broom
Candle
Carabiner Walk
Clock
Cobra
Duo Sit
Goldline Joust
Hopping Joust
Impulse
One Belay-Gotcha
Rat Tail-Gotcha
Red Baron Stretch
Ski Pole Slalom
Soccer Frisbee

The New Games Book
Catch the Dragon's Tail
Fox and Squirrel
Go Tag
Human Pinball
Lap Game
Smaug's Jewels
Standoff

Silver Bullets
Balloon Frantic
Boop
Bottoms Up
Circle the Circle
Comet Ball
Double Dutch
Everybody's Up
Fire in the Hole
Frantic
Group Juggling
Hoop Relay
Mine Field
Paul's Balls
Popsicle Push-Up
Rodeo Throw
Tattoo
Toss-A-Name Game

Bag of Tricks
Frisbee Shootout
Rope Push
Row Boat Stretch
Simplistic Tag
Slow-Motion Push
Triggers Toy

Cooperative Sports and Games
Blup Blup Up Up
Frozen Tak
Gesture Name Game
Hop-A-Long
Long Jump
Push 'em Into Balance

Hospital Tag
Moon Ball
Physics Phantasy
Quail Shooter's Delight
Smoke Stack
Texas Big Foot
Two in a Row

BY LEVEL

High School Level
Bottoms Up
Fox and Squirrel
Frisbee Shootout
Hoop Relay
Human Pinball
Impulse
Lap Game
One Belay-Gotcha
Popsicle Push-Up
Simplistic Tag
Soccer Frisbee
Texas Big Foot

All Levels
Add on Tag	Goldline Joust	Smoke Stack
Aerobic Tag	Group Juggling	Standoff
Balance Broom	Hop-a-Long	Tattoo
Boop	Hopping Joust	Triggers Toy
Bottoms Up	Hospital Tag	Turnstile
Circle the Circle	Human Pin Ball	Two in a Row
Clock	Moon Ball	
Cobra	Paul's Balls	
Double Dutch	Push 'em into Balance	
Duo Sit	Quail Shooter's Delight	
Everybody's It	Rope Push	
Fire in the Hole	Row Boat Stretch	
Frantic	Slow-Motion Push	
Go Tag	Smaug's Jewels	

Adapted from: © 1988, Project Adventure, Inc., Schoel, Prouty, and Radcliffe.
Used by permission.

DE-INHIBITIZER ACTIVITIES

Cowstails and Cobras

Bump
Dog Shake
Hog Call
Python Pentathlon
Yells

Silver Bullets

Funny Face
Inch Worm
Samurai

100 Ways to Enhance Self-Concept

Card Game
Guess Who I Am

The New Games Book

Prui

Cooperative Sports and Games

Wring the Dishrag

BY LEVEL

High School Level

Card Game
Dog Shake
Wring the Dishrag
Yells

All Levels

Bump
Funny Face
Guess Who I Am
Hog Call
Inch Worm
Prui
Python Pentathlon
Samurai

Adapted from: © 1988, Project Adventure, Inc., Schoel, Prouty, and Radcliffe.
Used by permission.

<u>Features:</u>

Activities involve some emotional and physical risk which may arouse some
   discomfort and frustration.
Success and failure are less important than trying and making a good effort.
Fun activities allow participants to view themselves asmore capable and
confident in front of others.
A cooperative and supportive atmosphere tends to encourage participants
   and increase confidence for all members in the group.

Trust and Empathy Activities

<u>Objectives:</u>

To provide an opportunity for group members to trust their physical and emotional
safety with others by attempting a graduated series of activities which involve taking some
physical and/or emotional risks.

<u>Features:</u>

Involves group interaction both physically and verbally.
Generally involves fun, but some fear as well.
Involves the support and cooperation of group members to care of the safety of
   others.
Risk taking occurs at many levels in most of the trust activities.
The development of trust occurs within the group gradually.
Trust activities are chosen with the intent of building trust; basic trust activities are
   initially chosen and can be performed repeatedly to reinforce and ensure the
   safety of group members.

Communication Activities

<u>Objectives:</u>

To provide an opportunity for group members to enhance their ability and skill to
communicate thoughts, feelings, and behaviors more appropriately through activities
which emphasize listening, verbal, and physical skills in the group decision making
process.

<u>Features:</u>

Physical activity, verbal interaction and discussion are major components in the
   sharing of ideas.
The solving of the problem is the established goal. Some frustration is generally
   evident in the solving of the problem.
Leadership abilities and skills usually evolve from participants within the group.
Most activities require at least five members.

TRUST AND EMPATHY ACTIVITIES

Cowstails and Cobras
Belaying
Blindfold Soccer
Hickory Jump
Trust Drive
Trust Falls from Perch
Trust Pass
Yurt Circle

Bag of Tricks
Blindfold High Events
Ladder Climb
Life Line
Things You Like To Do
Values Clarification

Unknown Origin
Airplane
Circle Pass
Elevated Trust Walk
Levitation
Pitch Pole
Rolling Cannonball
Three-Person Trust Fall
Two-Person Trust Fall

**Cooperative Sports
and Games Book**
Circle of Friends

Silver Bullets
Blindfold Tube-E-Cide
Compass Walk
Human Camera
Human Ladder
Sherpa Walk
Yeah, But

BY LEVEL

High School Level

Belaying
Blindfold High Events
Blindfold Soccer
Elevated Trust Walk
Hickory Jump
Human Ladder
Ladder Climb
Levitation
Life Line
Pitch Pole
Rolling Cannonball
Sherpa Walk
Things You Like To Do
Trust Drive
Two-Person Trust Fall
Yeah, But

All Levels

Blindfold Tube-E-Circle
Circle Pass
Human Camera
Three Person Trust Fall
Trust Falls from Perch
Trust Pass
Yurt Circle

Adapted from: ©1988, Project Adventure, Inc., Schoel, Prouty, and Radcliffe.
Used by permission.

COMMUNICATION ACTIVITIES

Cowstails and Cobras
All Aboard
Blindfold Paragon
Happy Landing
Tangle
Traffic Jam
Trolley

Silver Bullets
Body English
Circle
Body English
Bridge It
Say What
T. P. Shuffle
Tusker
Unholy Alliance
Zig Zag

The New Games Book
Aura
Islan
Rock-Paper-Scissors

100 Ways to Enhance Self-Concept
Mirroring
Reflective Listening
Statues
Partners

Unknown Origin
Murder Mystery
Non-Verbal Obstacle Course

Values Clarification
Alligator River
Who's to Blame

Bag of Tricks
Rain

Cooperative Games and Sports
Balloon Bucket
Blanketball
Blizzard
Carry On
Partners
Tug of Peace

BY LEVEL

High School Level

Alligator River
Bridge It
Mirroring
Murder Mystery
Rain
Say What
Statues
Who's to Blame

All Levels

Add-On-Tag
All Aboard
Aura
Blanketball
Blindfold Polygon
Body Englis
Non-Verbal Obstacle Course
Reflective Listening
Rock-Paper-Scissors
T.P. Shuffle
Traffic Jam
Trolley
Tusker
Unholy Alliance
Zig Zag

Adapted from: ©1988, Project Adventure, Inc., Schoel, Prouty, and Radcliffe.
Used by permission.

Decision Making/Problem Solving Activities

Objectives:

To provide an opportunity for group members to effectively communicate, cooperate, and compromise with each other through trial-and-error participation in a graduated series of problem solving activities that range from the more simply solved to the more complex.

Features:

Physical activity and verbal communication are involved in order to solve stated problems.

Arousing a higher level of frustration teaches that patience is a virtue.

Activities demand that group members can demonstrate an ability to listen, cooperate, and compromise.

Leadership roles evolve in the attempt to solve the stated problem or reach the stated goal.

Trial-and-error approach to learning is most often employed by the group in the problem solving/decision making process.

Social Responsibility Activities

Objectives:

To provide a setting wherein group participants can build upon previous gains in areas of acquaintance, trust, communications, and decision making, to develop skills in assessing and working effectively with the strengths and weaknesses of individuals in a group.

Features:

Success in these activities is somewhat dependent upon individuals being able to learn how to support and encourage each other's efforts.

Activities tend to help participants learn the value of thinking and planning ahead rather than reacting in an impulsive and random manner.

Activities tend to emphasize that participants in the group communicate and cooperate verbally and physically.

Activities help participants develop skills in assessing problems and formulating solutions.

Activities help relate the group to the world "outside" in an empathetic and concerned manner.

Activities tend to help individuals and the group identify and develop leadership in the group.

DECISION MAKING/PROBLEM SOLVING ACTIVITIES

Cowstails and Cobras
The Amazon
The Beam
Board Stretch
Diminishing Load
Electric Fence
Emergency
Four Pointer
Hanging Teeter Totter
Infinite Circle
Initiative Run
Jelly Roll
Low Swinging Log
Nitro Crossing
Reach for the Sky
Stranded
Ten Member Pyramid
Tin Shoe
Vertical Log and Tire
The Wall

Silver Bullets
A-Frame
Diminishing Load
  Problem
Group Juggling
Mohawk Walk
Pick and Choose
Punctured Drum
Ship Wreck
Soft Walk
Spider Web
T.P. Shuffle
T.T. Log
Touch My Can
Two by Four

BY LEVEL

High School Level
A-Frame
The Amazon
Diminishing Load Problem
Group Juggling
Nitro Crossing
Reach for the Sky
Two by Four
Vertical Log and Tire
The Wall

All Levels
4 Pointer
10 Member Pyramid
The Beam
Board Stretch
Electric Fence
Emergency
Initiative Run
Jelly Roll
Low Swinging Log
Mohawk Walk
Pick and Choose
Punctured Drum
Soft Walk
Spider Web
Stranded
T.P. Shuffle
T.T. Log
Tin Shoe
Touch My Can

Adapted from: © 1988, Project Adventure, Inc., Schoel, Prouty, and Radcliffe.
Used by permission.

SOCIAL RESPONSIBILITY ACTIVITIES

Cowstails and Cobras
Belaying
Fire Building
First Aid
Initiative Day
Rescue Techniques
Spotting
Winter Safety

The New Games Book
Siamese Soccer

Unknown Origin
Building a Rope Course
    Event
C.P.R.
Community Service Project
Environmental Protection
Fundraising Events
Litter Construction Projects

Values Clarification
Cave-In Simulation
Fall Out Shelter
"I Urge" Telegrams
Letters to the Editor
Sensitivity Modules
Values in Action

BY LEVEL

High School Level

Belaying
C.P.R.
Cave-In Simulation
Fire Building
First Aid
Rescue Techniques
Sensitivity Modules

All Levels

Building A Rope Course Event
Community Service Project
Environmental Protection
Fall Out Shelter
Fundrasing Events
"I Urge" Telegrams
Initiative Day
Letters to the Editor
Litter Construction Projects
Siamese Soccer
Spotting
Values in Action

PERSONAL RESPONSIBILITY ACTIVITIES

Cowstails and Cobras
2 Line Bridge
Balance Beam
Bosun's Chair
Breathe Easy
Burma Bridge
Commando Crawl
Criss Crotch
Dangle Do
Fidget Ladder
Flea Leap
Giant Swing
High Kitten Crawl
Inclined Log
Log Ladder
Low Swinging Log
Map and Compass
Pamper Pole
Prusiking
Rappelling
Rope Climb and Rope Ladder
Teaching Knots
Tension Traverse
Tire Traverse
Track Walk
Tyrolean Traverse
Wallenda Walk
Zip Wire

The New Games Book
Pina

100 Ways to Enhance Self-Concept
Moving in Mindfulness
Public Interview
Self Collage
Spontaneous Movement
Volunteering
Words That Describe Me

Values Clarification
Public Interview

Unknown Origin
High Commitment Jump
High Criss Cross Rope
Rock Climbing
Tree Climb

BY LEVEL

High School Level

2 Line Bridge
Commando Crawl
Dangle Do
High Commitment Jump
Map and Compass
Pamper Pole
Tire Traverse
Tyrolean Traverse
Wallenda Walk
Zip Wire

All Levels

Balance Beam
Bosun's Chair
Breathe Easy
Burma Bridge
Criss Crotch
Fidget Ladder
Flea Leap
Giant Swing
High Criss Cross Ropes
Inclined Log

Low Swinging Log
Pina
Rapelling
Rock Climbing
Rope Ladder
Teaching Knots
Track Walk
Tree Climb

Adapted from: © 1988, Project Adventure, Inc., Schoel, Prouty, and Radcliffe.
Used by permission.

147

Personal Responsibility Activities

<u>Objectives:</u>

To provide activities and initiatives of a somewhat more individualistic nature that challenge participants to develop persistence and resistance to frustration in attempting to reach a desired goal.

<u>Features:</u>

Most activities are "classic" rope course events that are both the most difficult and trying and the most exciting.

Activities help group members acknowledge individual and common reactions to fear, stress, and physical limitation.

Participation in these activities encourages group support for individual efforts.

Participation helps group members extend the limits of their self-perceived competence and builds self-confidence by successful completion of a difficult task.

Activities help group members to act on what they have learned about working together, supporting one another, and taking responsibility for one another's safety.

Many activities require some special equipment and construction and expert advice and training.

RESOURCE BOOKS

Canfield, J. and Wells, H. (1976). *100 ways to enhance self-concept in the classroom*. Englewood Cliffs, NJ: Prentice-Hall, Inc.

Fluegelman, A. (1976). *The New Games book*. Garden City, NY: Dolphin Books/Doubleday.

Fluegelman, A. (1981). *More New Games*. Garden City, NY: Dolphin Books/Doubleday.

Orlick, T. (1978). *The cooperative sports and games book*. New York, NY: Pantheon Books.

Rohnke, K. (1977). *Cowstails and cobras*. Hamilton, MA: Project Adventure, Inc. (This book is out of print and has been replaced by *Cowstails and cobras II*).

Rohnke, K. (1984). *Silver bullets*. Hamilton, MA: Project Adventure, Inc.

Rohnke, K. *Bag of tricks*. A Quarterly Newsletter, PO Box 77, Hamilton, MA 01936.

Simon, S.B.., Howe, L.W., and Kirschenbaum, H. (1972). *Values clarification: A handbook of practical strategies for teachers and students*. New York, NY: A & W Publishers, Inc.

Chapter Eighteen
PHYSICAL ACTIVITY AND EXERCISE

The Heart's Song

"This body is an amazing thing. Yet, after all the use, disuse, and abuse it will still make every effort it can to come through for you in the pinch. It's your heart that pleads first for your head, your mind, your will power to work in harmony. Yet, it is the worldly preoccupation of your mind that often does not listen to your heart's song; a song of love, understanding, joy, gentleness, compassion, hope ... a song of wisdom, a song of health."

Author unknown

"Every man is a builder of a temple, called his body ... We are all sculptors and painters, and our material is our flesh and blood and bone."

Henry David Thoreau

Physical exercise is essential in every person's life. Exercise in some form should take place every day. However, this often causes a problem, BOREDOM. It is important to have a variety of exercises so a person does not get bored, discouraged, and quit.

CD persons "wish" for a "fit body." Through physical activity and individual exercises this wish can become a reality, but it takes time, effort, and "stick-to-itiveness." One means is to have a written contract in which the person set goals and dates to achieve the goals. For some reason, if something is in writing it becomes more of a commitment. Another technique is to put a chart on the wall (at the facility or at home), which can be checked as something is achieved. These strategies give a person proof and pride in progress.

Physical games are an excellent source for exercise. New Games, basketball, soccer, volleyball, tag/flag football, frisbee, tag, and relays are some examples. Other activities are biking, roller skating, hiking, walking, jogging, going up and down stairs several times, jumping rope, dancing, and swimming. These activities increase cardiovascular functioning. Almost every section of this book has instructions for physical games.

Along with games, an individual exercise program should be developed. This program depends on the individual's condition, interests, and resources. Suggested exercises include:

low impact aerobics	jump rope
stationary bike	jumping jacks
regular bike	situps/modified pushups
rowing machine	stretching
weight lifting	walking
jogging	running

Fun and Motivational Exercises

Line Dances: Teach a few basics — change the music and reverse.

Crazy Dances: Combine segments of chicken dance, hokey pokey, bunny hop, la raspa.

Mimic Dances: Mimic different recreational activities to beat of music.

Hula Hoops: Roll a hoop down the floor. How many times can you run around it? Keep a hula hoop going (around your waist) for two minutes.

Knee Tap: Tap outside of partner's knees as they try to tap yours. Change focus by saying "You got me" instead of "I gottcha."

Overhead Arm Wrestling: Grip partner's wrist and try to tap top of partner's head with free hand or with gripped wrist.

Situps: Face partner, sit on each other's feet. One partner lies down, holding a ball, which he or she releases when coming to a sitting position. At same time, other partner is going to a lying position, and must catch the ball on the way down. Then that partner starts to a sitting position, releasing the ball on the way up. (It is like a teeter totter motion.)

Back to Back: Stand back to back and hook elbows with partner. Sit down, and come back to a standing position. Add two or more persons, hook elbows, sit down and stand up. Add four more persons, etc.

Other motivational exercise activities can be found in *Cowstails and Cobras II* (1989), pp. 30 - 50.

EXERCISE INTEREST CHECKLIST

It is well known that exercise is of benefit to everyone. Choosing which exercise to do is not an easy task! It depends on present physical condition, doctor recommendations (if necessary), personal likes and dislikes, etc.

Here's a list of choices. Put a "**P**" (present) in the first box if you presently do this two or more times each week. Put an "**F**" (future) in the second box if you are going to continue doing this or are considering doing this one or two times each week in the future.

☐☐ Jogging	☐☐ Bowling	☐☐ Baseball / Softball
☐☐ Walking	☐☐ Yardwork	☐☐ Roller / Ice-Skating
☐☐ Running	☐☐ Tennis	☐☐ Soccer
☐☐ Swimming	☐☐ Golf	☐☐ Volleyball
☐☐ Bicycling	☐☐ Weight Lifting	☐☐ Football
☐☐ Dancing	☐☐ Stretching	☐☐ Basketball
☐☐ Aerobics	☐☐ Aquatics	☐☐ _____
☐☐ Downhill Skiing	☐☐ Yoga	☐☐ _____
☐☐ Cross Country Skiing	☐☐ Work out Machines	☐☐ _____
☐☐ Water Skiing	☐☐ Racquetball	☐☐ _____

List of "P"s

_____
_____
_____
_____
_____

List of "F"s

_____
_____
_____
_____
_____

List 3 "**F**"s that you are not doing presently and identify what you'll need to do to GET STARTED.

1. _____
2. _____
3. _____

© 1989 Wellness Reproductions Inc.

Source: © 1989, *Life Management Skills*. Reproducible activity handouts created for facilitators. Available from Wellness Reproductions, Inc. 1-800-669-9208.

151

Chapter Nineteen
NUTRITION

Nutrition is an important component in the rehabilitation process. Most CD persons are not aware of or do not eat nutritional meals. Usually a nurse will give the lectures on nutrition. The TR staff can follow up on these lectures with the following activities:

1. Give each group identical advertisement flyers from a local chain (check list so that a variety of healthy foods are available) and a set budget. Have them plan a family meal, picnic, or special holiday meal.

2. Bring in a large selection of healthy and junk foods. Divide into groups and have members decide what they'd buy if they had $5 and were hungry. Then give them nutrition guides and have a race to see which team can come up with certain nutrient levels the fastest. Then have them discuss how certain foods are healthier choices than others.

3. Divide into groups and give each group a nutritional guide from a fast food chain (McDonald's, Wendy's, Burger King, Taco Bell, Kentucky Fried Chicken, Domino's Pizza Hut). Have them put together the least and most healthy meals possible and then report to the rest of the group.

4. Have them play The Price Is Right. Have lots of grocery items and have clients do fun pricing guessing games. Include the "Four Basic Food Groups" and "calorie content" guessing activities. Have fresh fruits and vegetables packaged in fun ways as prizes.

5. Give them pamphlets about the four food groups, then give them each a card with one of the four food groups on it. Have them seated equi-distant from you. Reach into the bag and pull out an item from one of the food groups. Everyone from that food group runs up and tries to be the first person to get their card placed on an X on the table. That person then becomes the person to pull the next food item out of the sack. Have some tricky items like jello, candy and pop and educate them about foods not belonging to one of the main four food groups.

6. Divide them into four categories and give them paper and pencil. Give them a food category. Then, using Scrabble tiles (or cards with letters on them), turn one over. Groups have one minute to list as many foods as they can that fall in that group and start with that letter. Teams get one point for every answer that no one else has. Have a nutrition guide handy for officiating. At end of program, have prizes from four food groups (peanuts, cheese, grapes, and popcorn) and let first place pick first, second goes second, etc.

7. Have them prepare healthy snacks for an upcoming party. Provide them with ideas and literature about making healthy, attractive party snacks. Encourage them to be open to new ideas and to help prepare snacks they might not like but others might try.

8. Have them prepare nonalcoholic party drinks. Give them ideas and literature telling about all the different options. Supply them with ice, blenders, fruit, sodas, etc.

FOOD GROUP REVIEW

and

Some healthy examples of each group

PROTEIN

MILK

dried beans   cheese

peanut butter   cottage cheese

meats   yogurt

dried peas   ice cream

eggs   milk

lentils   pudding

cheese

fish

fowl

Other: _____

_____

_____

_____

2

2

Minimum Servings Per Day

4

Other: _____

_____

_____

_____

Other: _____

_____

_____

Other: _____

_____

_____

rice   banana

pasta   grapes

muffins   strawberries

cereal   grapefruit

oats   peaches

breads   carrots

bran   broccoli

potatoes

spinach

BREADS & CEREAL

FRUITS & VEGETABLES

SAMPLE

Source: © 1989, *Life Management Skills*. Reproducible activity handouts created for facilitators. Available from Wellness Reproductions, Inc. 1-800-669-9208.

Chapter Twenty
OUTDOOR RECREATION

Millions of Americans flock to the out of doors for fun, adventure, education, enjoyment, and renewal of the spirit. Outdoor recreation offers unique values that should be experienced by everyone. The outdoors with its lore, history, beauty, color and natural resources provides opportunities to camp, picnic, hike, bike, fish, hunt, snow and water ski, boat, horseback ride, mountain climb, study the stars, collect natural materials, observe birds and animals, spectate or participate in sports and games, and experience the beauty of nature.

There is a tremendous diversity in outdoor recreation. A few activities are suggested in this section of the book. However, look throughout the book for activities that are done in the out of doors.

High adventure recreation has become popular. It involves rope courses, rock climbing/rappelling, white water rafting, kayaking, sky diving, scuba diving, and other activities involving risk.

Outdoor adventure programming has become a respected treatment modality for CD persons.

> Through the use of strategically structured, increment high adventure activities (i.e., rock climbing, rappelling, whitewater rafting, backpacking, canoeing, and initiative courses) participants have the opportunity to transform themselves from a self defeating, failure orientation to a self empowered, confident lifestyle. As group members internalize the lessons learned from these living metaphors, they begin to set goals for themselves and to take responsibility for their behaviors. Problem solving skills are developed by continually providing tasks that are physically and psychologically challenging and that can be mastered repeatedly to enhance the participant's feelings of worth. Building self esteem is one of the cornerstones of addiction treatment and adventure therapy. (Phelps, 1989, p. 2)

The most widely used resources for high adventure and outdoor adventure programs are *Project Adventure, Cowstails and Cobras, Cowstails and Cobras II,* and *Silver Bullets.* Ideas for interesting family hikes include:

Rainbow Hike: Find and list as many colors in nature as possible, especially after rain.

Monogram Hike: Find three or more nature objects beginning with your initials.

Incher Hike: Collect as many objects as possible that are one inch high, wide, around, long, etc.

<u>Stop, Look, and Listen Hike:</u> Hike for five minutes. Stop and each person tell what he or she saw or heard.

<u>Curiosity Hike:</u> Find some odd or curious object such as bark, stone, etc. Use imagination to tell what animal, etc. the object represents.

<u>Nature Hike:</u> Observe birds, insects, land animals, rocks and minerals, trees and shrubs, water animals, and wild plants.

<u>Camera Hike:</u> Bring a camera, take pictures along the way, choosing subjects which are important and characteristic.

(Ideas above taken from Camp Fire, Girl Scouts, and Boy Scouts camping activities.)

<u>Family Scavenger Hunt:</u> Keep family within hearing distance of each other. Give each member a list of nature objects to find. Suggestions: pine cone, white stone, maple leaf, something red, something that spoils the looks of the scenery, one crooked stick, caterpillar or worm, feather, seed, something a bird would eat, pine needle. This could be a 30-minute, concentrated activity, or it could be an all day, "do it at will" activity.

Chapter Twenty-One
VALUES CLARIFICATION

Not everything that is faced can be changed,
But nothing can be changed until it is faced.
James Baldwin

"Values are the established ideals of life; objects, customs, ways of acting, etc., that the members of a given society regard as desirable" (The World Book Dictionary). Values can involve estimating the worth of; to think highly of; regard highly. Value can also mean to judge the worth correctly: "I value your friendship." Values can be monetary, psychological, social, or culturally-related.

Values clarification is the process or procedure that makes you aware of your own values. It is nonjudgmental. It is a set of strategies that help you clarify your attitudes toward everything. It helps you define how you really feel.

We live in an ever changing world, with ever changing values. We are forced to make choices based on the values we have, but frequently we are not clear about our own values. There are many situations that cause a conflict in values: for example, you want to make good grades in school, but you don't want to alienate your peers. The idea of "conflict in values" or "unclear values" doesn't mean only the traditional values of honesty, truth, beauty, love, friendship, and justice but it includes time management, money, peer pressure, respect, health, work, and leisure. It is important that we recognize our own values and understand why we feel certain ways. We must also have the right to express our own values.

Clarifying values is difficult for CD persons to do. They have been "out of things" and it is hard for them to think through on something. Sometimes persons have not had role models or situations in which they could develop values. TR staff need to assist persons in clarifying values. There are many different ways in which to do this. The following exercises will aid in this process.

Excellent resources for values clarification materials are:

Simon, S.B., Howe, L.W., and Kirschenbaum, H. (1972). *Values Clarification: A Handbook of Practical Strategies for Teachers and Students*. New York: Hart Publishing Company.

McDowell, C.F. (1976). *Leisure Counseling: Selected Lifestyle Processes*. Eugene, OR: University of Oregon.

HOW TO VALUE YOURSELF

1. Don't demand perfection from yourself. Set realistic goals that you can and want to achieve.

2. Reward, comfort, and love yourself. You're OK!

3. You have the right to decide who, how, and what you want to be without making excuses, justifying, or saying, "I'm sorry." You are responsible for everything you do unless you are physically overpowered. So it's your life and what happens in it is up to you.

4. Refuse to be manipulated by other people's greed, helplessness, or anger. So set limits. Say "no" when you mean "no." And confront those who try to manipulate you with "you should."

5. Check out your "should's to yourself." Is it something you want? OK. Something you have to do, like pay your bills? That's reality. But that's not a "should."

6. Recognize feelings of inadequacy and guilt for what they are —legacies from your parents and other adults. You can decide not to feel that way.

7. Be constructively selfish. In the long run, doing what is best for you is usually best for everyone concerned. Remember that no matter what you do, someone is not going to like it -so you have to risk being disliked, or even ending relationships, if you are going to function in your own best interests.

8. Recognize that there are limits to your power. You really control no more than 50% of a relationship — your half. Remember — you have the right to say "I don't understand" and even "I don't care."

9. Don't answer questions you don't want to answer. Questions are often threatening, demanding, manipulative -- especially the WHY and WHY NOT questions. Nowhere is it engraved in stone that you must answer questions.

10. Stay in the here-and-now and cope with reality. If you blame others or the world for your problems ... or if your behavior is aimed at making you feel better instead of solving your problems -- you are defending instead of coping. Every healthy person has problems and you do have the ability to cope with them.

What DO I Value ?

The degree to which we live by our own sense of values can greatly influence our self-satisfaction. When we say we hold a specific value in high regard, yet act in a manner which opposes this value, inner conflict can result.

List below your 5 highest values and note how they are *expressed* in your life and/or how they are *opposed*.

I value:	I *express* this by:	I *oppose* this by:
Loyalty	Keeping secrets. Defending my friends.	Gossiping. Not being there when my friends need me.
Classical Music	I go to concerts and listen to tapes while driving.	Watching TV every evening after work instead of putting on my records.
1.		
2.		
3.		
4.		
5.		

Source: © 1989, *Life Management Skills*. Reproducible activity handouts created for facilitators. Available from Wellness Reproductions, Inc. 1-800-669-9208.

The following activities can be used to facilitate values clarification. You can use activities on an individual basis, where participants fill out the sheet, or you can use them as a group activity where you ask the questions of the group and each individual raises his or her hand when you read the choices the second time.

REACTION STATEMENTS

In the following problems, which solution would you choose?

You are married and have your own children. Your mother dies and your father is old. What would you do?
a. Invite him to live in your home.
b. Place him in a home for aged.
c. Get him an apartment by himself.

You have epilepsy. Your seizures are under control. You are being interviewed for a job in recreation. You really want the job. Interviewer asks you if you have any disabilities. You say:
a. "No"
b. "Yes" and explain
c. "You have no legal right to ask me"

Joe has been mentally ill. He went berzerk and tried to kill his mother. He has been under psychiatric care and is now considered "normal." He is back in school and asks you for a date. Your response is:
a. "No way"
b. "Maybe" (but only one time as a courtesy)
c. "Why not" (he is a fellow human being and just got off the track for awhile)

You are at a dance. Someone who is blind asks you to dance. You would:
a. Say, "no" and feel guilty
b. Say, "yes" and enjoy it
c. Say, "yes" and feel embarrassed

Your neighbor, who is a very good friend, physically abuses her child. You would:
a. Report it, not leaving your name
b. Talk with her about it
c. Not get involved

RANK ORDER

Rank the following statements according to how you feel about them.

Which person is the most stupid?
a. Boy wears helmet when riding motorcycle, but does not buckle it.
b. Lady has small lump in breast, but is too embarrassed to go to the doctor.
c. Man has lung cancer, but keeps on smoking.

159

You have been in a terrible car accident. You would have the most trouble adjusting to the loss of:

    a. Eyesight
    b. Hearing
    c. A limb

VALUE VOTING

You will put a value on the following, according to how you feel. If you are very much for the statement — raise your hand and wave. If you are against the statement — put thumbs down and shake hands. If you do not want to commit yourself or are noncommittal — cross your arms.

    a. How many want to free fall and parachute safely?
    b. How many have told someone he/she has bad breath — since Christmas?
    c. You are in a record store and see a person steal a record. How many would stop the rip-off?

When you have gone through several of these strategies, ask yourself, or have others ask themselves:

1. Are you satisfied with how you are spending you time?
2. What changes would you like to make in how you are spending your time?
3. Is there anything you can do to change how you are spending your time?

Leisure Values

The following exercises are helpful in clarifying values concerning an individual's leisure.

1. What do you get out of the following leisure experience? What needs does it fulfill, or what kind of satisfaction does it elicit?

    a. Jogging (example: sense of freedom, conditioning)
    b. Shopping
    c. Visiting

2. What do you do in leisure that gives you the following feelings?

    a. Excitement
    b. Boredom

3. What do you do in leisure that gives a feeling of accomplishment or satisfaction?

4. On a scale of 1 - 5 (5 being highest) how would you rate the following experiences?

  a. Dancing
  b. Dining out
  c. Attending a party
  d. Watching a sunset with someone you like
  e. Fishing
  f. Visiting with a friend
  g. Playing golf
  h. Watching a baseball game
  i. Canoeing down a river

5. Rank answers in order of personal preference.

  a. Which is most important in a friendship? (rank 1, 2, 3)
     ___ Loyalty   ___ Generosity   ___ Honesty

  b. Which would you most like to improve? (rank 1, 2, 3)
     ___ Your looks ___ The way you use your time
     ___ Your social life

  c. Which do you think is the most religious thing to do on Sunday? (rank 1, 2, 3, 4)

     ___ Go to church and hear a good sermon
     ___ Listen to some peaceful music
     ___ Go for a long walk alone
     ___ Have a big family breakfast
     ___ Other

  d. You suddenly inherited a large sum of money. Would you? (rank 1, 2, 3)

     ___ Continue in your present job and activities
     ___ Really live it up
     ___ Share your wealth through charities, educational trust funds, etc.
     ___ Other

It is obvious that choices will be different. Persons value things in different ways. "Different strokes for different folks" is an appropriate statement here. There is no right or wrong in the above choices, it is up to the individual. These choices force people to look at how they value things.

Chapter Twenty-Two
STRESS

Stress is a realistic part of life. The demands of our physical and social environment require that every person learn to adjust or adapt his or her behavior constantly. By subjecting ourselves to stressful situations, we force ourselves to adapt/adjust. Fortunately, many stressful situations don't exceed our ability to adjust and, therefore, lead to adaptations that are productive and positive. When stress leads to a pleasant or positive experience it is called *eustress*. When excessive demands are placed on us, the experience is unpleasant and we experience *distress*. Distress can be physical or emotional. Factors that determine the impact of emotional stress on a person include environmental conditions, the personality of the individual, and the perception of the stressor by the individual.

In dealing with stress, direct action involves eliminating the stressor , for example, a person irritates you and it is not necessary to be around this person, so you simply stay away from that individual. Another example would be when you have tried repeatedly to play golf and cannot master the skills. You become very stressed. Therefore, you would stop playing golf and replace it with another activity that gives you satisfaction, without stress.

However, sometimes it is not possible to eliminate a stressor, so direct control techniques are called into play. Direct control techniques involve analyzing the stressor and, recognizing that it cannot be eliminated, determining ways in which to deal with it. It should be noted that direct control techniques can be positive or negative. Two examples are as follows: Late afternoon is a stressful time because of restlessness and boredom. A negative direct control technique could be excessive drinking, which only creates other type of stresses. A positive control technique could involve calling a friend, walking in the park, or developing an exercise/fitness routine to be done during that time of day.

Another word used in some of the following exercises is "buffer." Buffers are those actions or activities that temporarily relieve stress. Persons must determine which buffers are the most effective for them individually. The term "quick stress reducers" is another term that can be used interchangeably with buffer.

Addicts are manipulators, masters of evasion, and con artists. They do not do well under stress. They become agitated when they get under pressure (real or imagined). They become physically or verbally abusive one minute, but if they realize they have lost control of a situation, they become charming. They try to control the situation.

Physical activity such as walking, volleyball, bowling, and darts can be used effectively to reduce stress. Other quick stress reducers include writing a letter to a friend, taking a bubble bath, smiling a lot, singing, listening to music, calling a friend, going shopping, saying hello to someone new, watching a sunrise or a sunset, reminiscing, playing like a child, laughing, relaxing.

A variety of activities can make persons aware of what stresses them and how they can individualize and respond to that stressor.

WHOLE PERSON STRESS INVENTORY

Fill in below with the following choices:
> 2 - Much of the time
> 1 - Sometimes
> 0 - Never

Consider the items below as they function <u>during</u> high stress periods:

Mental
___ Do you have a hard time remembering where you left things?
___ Are your conversational skills limited to work or problems?
___ Do you have a hard time concentrating on reading?
___ Does your mind feel sluggish?

Social
___ Is leisure time alone rather than with a friend or friends?
___ Are you tense and uncomfortable with friends and family?
___ Do you dislike mixing with people socially?
___ Are the holidays a nuisance and an interruption to your life?

Physical
Do you have:
___ Ulcers or indigestion?
___ Insomnia, accident proneness?
___ Frequent eyestrain, headaches, body aches?
___ Fatigue, lethargy, no energy?

Sensory
___ Do you fail to notice the odors of plants and flowers?
___ Do you pass from home to work and not notice things?
___ Do you fail to taste food?
___ Do you fail to notice the warmth of the sun or coolness of the air and to enjoy these things?

Spirit
___ Do you tend to follow others, go along with the ideas of everyone else?
___ Do you fail to take time to think about your life?
___ Are you often in a down mood at work or home?
___ Do you wake up in a depressed mood?

STRESS PROBLEM SOLVING

1. What are the major stressors for you now?

2. Pick the most important one for you at this time in your life. Describe it in more detail.

3. Do you have the motivation to handle this stressor?

4. Who is responsible for this stressor? You? Someone else? Combination of both?

5. What is the cause of this stressor (e.g., frustration, threat, conflict, Type A behavior)?

6. Is direct action (eliminate the stressor) possible or will you have to rely on direct control techniques (adapt to the stressor)?

7. If direct action is possible, what are the alternatives?

HOW DO YOU COPE?

Next to each action below, put the number(s) of the reasons why you did or might do it. Try to think of reasons why you might have started doing it, as well as reasons for continuing it. Even if some actions do not apply to you, fill in reasons if you can imagine yourself doing the actions.

Feel free to add items to either list.

When you have completed the checklist, circle three or four actions that have at least six reasons assigned to them. You may want to think about these to see the importance of such actions in your life.

Actions

A. Run away
B. Drink colas
C. Have a drink
D. Watch TV
E. Play a musical instrument
F. Have a place for everything
G. Eat pastry on Sunday
H. Walk the dog
I. Go to religious services
J. Play a sport
K. Sunbathe
L. Daydream
M. Put things off
N. Do nothing
O. Sleep late
P. Take tranquilizers
Q. Take vitamins
R. Fly a kite
S. Take chances
T. Have a savings account
U. Hang around with friends
V. Avoid being late
W. Buy clothes
X. Make people laugh
Y. Read a book
Z. Have a routine

Reasons

1. Makes me feel good
2. Reduces tension
3. Puts order in my life
4. Gives me something uniquely mine
5. Perks me up
6. Calms me down
7. Provides a change of pace
8. Gives me social acceptance
9. Gives me a sense of well-being
10. Makes me anxious if I do not do it
11. Makes me feel guilty if I don't do it
12. Makes me feel "square" if I don't do it
13. Makes me feel powerful
14. I have to - it is one of life's givens
15. My parents did it
16. My friends approve of it
17. _____
18. _____
19. _____
20. _____
21. _____
22. _____
23. _____
24. _____
25. _____
26. _____
27. _____
28. _____
29. _____
30. _____

BUFFERS

Select and try under each category two buffers that you feel would be effective for you in reducing stress. If these do not work, try others until you come up with an effective combination.

Physical Buffers

___ Massage and heat.

___ Stretching exercise to pull tightness out if done slowly.

___ Releases. Moving rapidly to music, jogging, swimming or biking at an aerobic pace for YOUR heart.

___ A warm bath.

___ Water therapies such as jacuzzi, sauna, swim, foot bath.

___ Neck rolls, shoulder shrugs.

___ Lie for 15 minutes with feet elevated.

___ Learn to recognize neuromuscular tension is a body part and deliberately tighten up and then let that tension go.

___ Autogenics. Learning to progressively make body areas feel heavy and relaxed.

___ Try to "let go" and continue letting go beyond the point of zero tension. Start at head and work down. Progressive relaxation.

___ Rest. Take relaxation "cat naps" during tension build-up.

___ Check for tension throughout the day. Make tension check plan.

Mental Buffers

___ Practice positive self-talk. Eliminate negative self-talk.

___ Do some fantasy relaxation. Imagine yourself floating on a cloud or river. See yourself in a favorite place.

___ Contemplation. Meditation. Prayer.

___ Sit in a beautiful area -- by the ocean, stream, in garden, art gallery.

___ Be aware of soothing colors. Blue and green are soothing.

___ Have cards, posters in your visible environment as relaxation reminders.

___ Problem solve. Use paper and pencil. Write down problem, your negative response, a rational response or responses.

Behavior and Activity Buffers

___ Recreation in the outdoors (strongly recommended as sedative).

___ Find a craft. Crafts can be a lightning rod for stress.

___ Get away. Drive somewhere. Bike somewhere. Walk somewhere.

___ Change your environment and get out of the old stress tracks.

___ Have a conversation with a nonabrasive friend.

___ Watch dogs to see how other dogs can make their hackles rise. Yours do, too.

___ Learn to savor food. Have candles, music, decore. Eat slowly. Talk.

___ Listen to music as a mood lifter or soother.

FOUR-STAR BUFFERS

Supremes to Make Your Body Sing.

___ LAUGHTER

A good, hearty, muscle flexing, lung expanding, face reddening, tear squirting, fall-on-the-floor-special of a laugh. You feel warm, wild, and wonderful. Very physical! Very oxygenating!

___ COMPLIMENTS

If you BELIEVE what you are told when given a compliment you will feel that norepinephrine in action. You may blush on the outside, but a heartily felt compliment will flush you on the inside as well. Pity the non-believer! Such are losing a great health opportunity.

___ GOOD NEWS/ACHIEVEMENT

Completing a class, finishing a test or final, finishing anything, including the day or week, being a contestant on a game show, winning at ANYTHING. Good news and completions are everywhere. Some people are very capable of CELEBRATING these multitudinous moments of life and their body, mind, and surroundings benefit!

___ POSITIVE THINKING/EMOTIONAL PARTICIPATION

Both mind and emotions are involved. It's cheering contemplation, reading inspirational material, talking to an upbeat person. You both LIKE and LOVE a friend, idea, pet. It is that high feeling when you see a poster you respond to, hear some music for love. It's Monday Night Football for some, La Traviata for others. It's a mind/heart UP response.

___ RISK RECREATION

This behavior includes reaching out to meet someone you don't know, riding a horse, water skiing, snow skiing, theme park rides, performing before others.

Adapted from © 1986, C. O'Connor

THE STRESS DIET

BREAKFAST

1/2 Grapefruit
1 Piece Whole Wheat Toast
3 oz. Skim Milk

LUNCH

4 oz. Lean Broiled Chicken Breast
1 Cup Steamed Zucchini
1 Oreo Cookie
Herb Tea

MID-AFTERNOON SNACK

Rest of the Package of Oreo Cookies
1 Quart of Rocky Road Ice Cream
1 Jar of Hot Fudge

DINNER

2 Loaves Garlic Bread
Large Mushroom and Pepperoni Pizza
Large Pitcher of Beer
3 Milky Ways
Entire Frozen Cheesecake, eaten directly from the freezer

... Author Unknown (could
be any one of us!)

Chapter Twenty-Three
RELAXATION

One major way to cope with stress and tension is through relaxation. Tension is the response to both positive and negative stress.

Sleep disturbances are often evident in addictive persons due to the onset of withdrawal symptoms after two to four hours of sleep. Persons wake up agitated and anxious. Before treatment the usual response was to take a drink or drugs to get back to sleep. Even after detoxification, these symptoms occur. The persons must find alternatives for the drugs. Again, some form of relaxation is effective.

Different types of relaxation include deep breathing, grounding, total/centering relaxation, and progressive relaxation. All methods should be tried and then the individual can determine which one, or combination of two or more, is most effective.

Relaxation is not a cure-all. It does not remove the problems, responsibilities, or worries, but it does allow them to be dealt with effectively through increased self-control.

Deep Breathing

Deep breathing encourages the participant to slowly use the full lung capacity without holding one's breath. This begins to calm the participant by centering thought on the body.

Instructions: Breathe in slowly through the mouth, feeling as though you are sucking through a straw. Breathe deeply, feel the diaphragm rise. Breathe slowly and evenly. Concentrate on the rise and fall of your chest.

Continue this from three to five minutes. Can be done in standing, sitting, or supine position.

Grounding

This technique should be conducted in a relatively quiet location with enough space to allow each person to move freely. The leader should instruct participants as follows:

Sometimes it feels good to feel yourself connected solidly to the ground, to be part of the Earth, like a tree. As you stand here, let your body become comfortable and still, relaxing your shoulders and your legs, moving a little until you feel a spot that feels good. Close your eyes — feel yourself as a tree growing out of the ground. (Pause 10 seconds)

Imagine your roots going deep down in the earth below your feet. (Pause 10 seconds)

Raise your arms and imagine them as branches. They are solidly connected to the trunk of the tree. The trunk goes into the roots, which are deep in the earth. (Pause 10 seconds)

Feel the energy flow from the tips of your branches to the trunk of the roots in the earth. (Pause 10 seconds)

169

You can use this feeling of being part of the Earth whenever you want to feel solid and connected; whenever you want to feel yourself part of the flow of energy through the Earth. Enjoy that feeling for as long as you want now. Then come back to your own speed.

Total/Centering Relaxation

Conduct in a quiet, comfortable place. Have persons select a space on the floor with a mat or a towel.

The leader should instruct the group as follows:

Lie on your back.
Breathe deeply. Center within your chest.
Reach across your chest. Grab both shoulders, pull together and let them settle on the floor.
Put your hands overhead, palms up.
Close your eyes.
Breathe deeply. Relax. Don't think of anything -- no problems, no school, just relax and concentrate on the rise and fall of your chest.

Legs are slightly apart, hips spread -- no strain on hips at all.

Let your jaw fall open slightly. Breath deeply and relax. Now raise one hand and put the back of it across your forehead, smoothing all the wrinkles, let the hand drop back on the floor. Feel the forehead go smooth -- no fluttering of the eyelids, just relax.

Concentrate on the rise and fall of the chest. Fingertips should be curled and relaxed. They should feel like they are floating.

Point your toes in and then let them flop out. Concentrate on the rise and fall of your chest -- no problems. Your whole body is floating. Breathe evenly and smoothly.

Now slowly -- without effort, move the head from side to side. Now let it fall to one side or the other.

Your whole body is floating. Breathe evenly and smoothly -- concentrate on the rise and fall of your chest.

Swing one leg over the other leg and slowly roll over onto your tummy.
Put hands down by hips, with elbows bent and fingers curled up. Point the chin into one shoulder. One side of the face should feel hard and flat -- the other side should be relaxed.
Breathe slowly and deeply.

Let the toes point in or out -- just so the pressure is off the buttocks.

You should have a very relaxed feeling in the shoulders and buttocks.

Breathe slowly.

170

Fingertips are floating.

You lie very relaxed on the floor -- feeling like you are slowly sinking into the floor - relax. Breathe deeply.

(Give one to two minutes) Slowly open your eyes, roll over, sit up -- still breathing deeply.

How do you feel? Get up gently. Move about slowly for a few minutes.

Progressive Relaxation

Progressive relaxation involves tensing and then relaxing each group of muscles in the body, progressing from head to toe, or from the feet upwards. Suggested sequence is the scalp, forehead muscles, muscles across the upper lip and cheeks, jaw muscles, chin and throat muscles, chest muscles, back muscles between shoulder blades, hand muscles, forearm and upper arm muscles, abdominal muscles, buttocks, upper leg muscles, calf muscles, toe and arch muscles. Persons can sit in a chair in a relaxed position, or they can lie down.

An example of groups of muscles:

Make a fist with your right hand and squeeze as tightly as possible. Hold it. Hold it (five to seven seconds). Relax. Can you feel the muscles "letting go?"

Tense the muscles in your upper right arm. Hold it. And relax. Feel the tension flowing out.

Complete this same sequence with the left hand and arm.

Chapter Twenty-Four
DECISION MAKING

Too often, important decisions that affect our lives are made unconsciously, without adequate analysis, and without attention to the emotions and feelings involved. We make decisions every day —"Should I go to work or go fishing?" "Should I go to class or sleep?" "Should I have a hamburger or a hot dog?" Decisions are not right or wrong. A decision is judged to be effective or ineffective by whether it produces satisfying or unsatisfying consequences.

Personal decision making enables one to reason through life situations, solve problems, and modify behavior. The person making decisions must be responsible for the consequences. Decision making involves values and the two go hand in hand.

Decision making is a process involving five steps:

1. Defining the problem
2. Looking at influences
3. Identifying alternatives
4. Looking at risks and results
5. Deciding, acting, and evaluating

Possible discussions for the steps would include:

1. DEFINING THE PROBLEM

Is it a problem? Whose? What specifically is the problem?

2. LOOKING AT INFLUENCES

Parental/Family — What do my parents/family think?

Peers — In what ways are attitudes of my friends putting pressure on my decisions? When is pressure helpful, harmful?

Legal — What are legal, social, cultural pressures?

Personal — Mood, state of mind, emotions? Do emotions help or hurt?

3. IDENTIFYING ALTERNATIVES

What possibilities are open? What facts are needed to weigh alternatives? What influences on each possibility?

4. LOOKING AT RISKS AND RESULTS

Examine different alternatives in light of what is likely to happen. What potential benefits and risks are going to occur? Are the payoffs worth the costs?

5. DECIDING, ACTING, AND EVALUATING

Look at past decisions to guide future actions. What decision did I make, and what action, thought, or feeling resulted? How satisfied am I with the decision? What cost did I expect from the decision? What did I have to give up? What payoff, or positive outcome, did I hope to get from the decision? What were the actual costs and payoffs? What would I do differently next time, or how would I make that decision now if I could turn back the clock and decide again?

CD persons must learn to make decisions based on the five- step decision making process. They need to learn the process and then practice making decisions on mock situations. This is not a one-time process, but needs to be practiced every day.

It is helpful to set up situations that are typical for CD persons. In this way they can be prepared for things that might occur.

Adapted: © 1982. *Decisions About Alcohol and Other Drugs: A Curriculum from Nebraska Schools*, by B. Riley and Ian Newman. Lincoln: University of Nebraska (NPCDA).

STEPS IN THE DECISION MAKING PROCESS

Divide clients into small groups. Give each group a set of "Steps in Decision Making Process," which have been cut into separate steps. Ask clients to work together to arrange slips in a sequence that they think would make a good decision making process.

(cut)- -

DEFINING THE PROBLEM

What is the problem?
Whose problem is it?
What information do I need to make a decision/solve the problem?

(cut)- -

LOOKING AT INFLUENCES

Who or what is influencing my decision?

(cut)- -

IDENTIFYING ALTERNATIVES

What choices do I have?

(cut)- -

LOOKING AT RISKS AND RESULTS

What will happen as a result of each possible choice?
What are the possible benefits?
What are the possible costs or negative outcomes?

(cut)- -

DECIDING, ACTING, AND EVALUATING

Given the possible outcomes, what choice looks best? What happens? Given what happened, what would I do differently next time?

(cut)- -

© 1982, *Decisions about Alcohol and Other Drugs: A Curriculum from Nebraska Schools,* by B. Riley, and Ian Newman. Lincoln: University of Nebraska (NPCADA).

DECISION MAKING SITUATIONS

Give one of the following situations to each group of 3 or 4 persons, or have the group make up some different situations for decision making.

Use the form titled Consequence Sheet (on the following page) to record three alternative decisions for each situation.

1. You have come home after work to an empty house. What do you do?

2. You have finished your work week and now have a two day break. You feel like celebrating and rewarding yourself for working hard and making it through. What do you do?

3. You are at a dance. Friends are going to parking lot for a "fix." They ask you to come along. What do you do?

4. You have just graduated from college. Your folks give you $2,000. You have been planning on going to graduate school. A group of your friends are going to Florida and ask you to go along. How do you use the money?

5. You have planned a whitewater raft trip down the Colorado River for the past year. You have a good guide. However, during the week before your planned trip there have been two tragic accidents on the river in which two persons were drowned. Do you go ahead with your trip? Alternatives?

6. You have gotten a sales job after being unemployed for two months. You have had a drinking problem in the past, but have been through treatment. Your boss invites you to dinner. The boss believes that drinking is part of the sales "picture" and is sure to suggest cocktails before dinner. What do you do?

CONSEQUENCE SHEET

For a problem, select three alternative solutions. List the positive and negative consequences for each.

Problem: _____

1. Possible Alternative: _____

Positive Consequences	Negative Consequences

2. Possible Alternative: _____

Positive Consequences	Negative Consequences

3. Possible Alternative: _____

Positive Consequences	Negative Consequences

MAKE A DECISION!

Category: Decision making
Supplies: Written instructions for each player
Age Level: Adolescent, adult
Time: 15 minutes
Objective: To use the decision making process

Description/Instructions: Because the car industry has run into difficult times, it is necessary to lay off two people from the marketing division. You are one of five persons on the personnel committee that makes the decisions on who will be laid off. From among the five persons described below, which two would you select. Why? What influenced your decision?

> - a 60-year-old man who is consistently in the top 10 for marketing ideas. Misses work often because of community services commitments.

> - a 38-year-old recovering alcoholic who completed treatment six months ago. She has missed three days of work since returning. She needs some motivation to develop new marketing ideas.

> - a 25-year-old man who has brilliant ideas but has difficulty on following through. Has been "cautioned" twice about "use of drugs" while on the job.

> - a 50-year-old woman who has worked her way up in the company over the past 28 years. She is consistent in her work, but is critical of other staff.

> - a 40-year-old man who has twins starting college. He was a mediocre worker until two years ago when he created a new marketing technique that has brought four new accounts to the company.

ROAD TO RECOVERY

Category: Decision making
Supplies: Large sheets of paper, pencils
Age Level: Adolescent, adult
Time: 50 minutes
Objectives: To decide on solutions for barriers
                To share goals

Description/Instructions: Have each participant individually draw his or her "Road to Recovery." The participants will identify what they need on the road, obstacles which may be anticipated, options or alternatives for obstacles. The participants should start the road from current point in recovery.

Processing: Allow each participant to share his or her "Road to Recovery."
Encourage participants to problem solve together.

FANTASY VACATION PLANNING

Category: Decision making
Supplies: 8 1/2 x 11 U.S. map, markers, pens
Age Level: Adolescent, adult
Time: 30 - 40 minutes
Objective: To help persons make decision on where they would vacation and why

Description/Instructions: Distribute a map of the United States to each participant. Each person is to designate a fantasy vacation within U.S. boundaries. Plot this vacation on the map. Pick five different leisure spots in five different states. Vacation will last two weeks, not counting travel time.

Processing: After each individual plots a vacation, split into groups of 4-5 people who will discuss decisions with group members. Each individual should explain why he or she decided on each vacation spot.

Chapter Twenty-Five
OPEN RECREATION

Within inpatient, outpatient, and community programs, leisure education sessions incorporate information on a variety of activities, as well as an opportunity for basic skill development in activities. All programming includes a variety of activities, so a person should be exposed to enough different types to decide what he or she would like to pursue.

Open recreation is the time when individuals can make a choice of activities in which they wish to participate. Open recreation offers opportunities for them to accept the responsibility for choices. They must think, choose, and follow through on taking part in activities. It does not mean that they are free to "do nothing."

Open recreation should start the process of selecting activities that, hopefully, will become part of the person's leisure lifestye.

The list of possible activities is endless. What gives satisfaction to one person may not be effective or appropriate for another. Categories of recreation are listed here, with the hope that this book and the references included at the end will provide a source of adequate variety within each category.

Kinds of activities include:

- aquatics
- arts and crafts
- care (plants, animals)
- communications (reading, writing, speaking, viewing)
- dance
- drama
- education
- hobbies
- music (singing, listening, playing instruments)
- nature and outdoor pursuits
- physical and mental fitness
- physical games, New Games
- social activities
- sports
- table games
- volunteerism

Chapter Twenty-Six
FAMILY ACTIVITIES

"A family system resembles a mobile ... The beauty of the mobile is in the balance and its flexibility ... It changes positions but always maintains connections with each part" (Wegschneider, 1979, pp. 36-37). The whole system moves to bring self into equilibrium.

In the family where there is chemical abuse, the whole organism shifts to bring balance, stability, and survival. Each family member adapts his or her behavior in the way that causes the least amount of personal stress. This struggle to maintain balance results in a dysfunctional family. Treatment programs are necessary for the family. They are not as intense as treatment for the CD individual, but they are an important part of the rehabilitation program.

Family Messages

Families generally have "written rules," which are usually "stated" to individual family members. Examples might be, "You can watch TV after you have finished your homework" or "You don't open other people's mail." Family members are aware of these rules because someone has told them verbally or in a message.

However, there are also "unwritten rules," which are not directly stated verbally or in messages. They are learned through observation of others, indirect verbal statements, or a person's own feelings of pride and protection for the family. Examples include:

1. Don't talk about family problems. Don't rock the boat.
2. Don't express feelings.
3. Don't be selfish (conveys message that your needs are not important).
4. It's not okay to play.
5. Don't trust others.
6. Keep adventurous play a secret.
7. A sense of humor is "silly."
8. "Covering up" is not really a lie.
9. Be successful/perfect.
10. You can handle anything.

Such unwritten rules, which are prevalent in the CD family, are very destructive to all concerned. Leisure and recreation have components that are helpful in eliminating the negative rules and replacing them with positive, constructive rules by which a family can live. Some of these components are positive self-concept, an informal way to express feelings, feeling of comfort in playing, cooperation and trust in other people, fun and laughter, ability to win or lose gracefully, and the fact that "it's okay to ask for help."

180

The co-dependents of drug addicts are subject to a whole series of defenses and feelings that need to be taken into consideration. These include:

Defenses (the outside):	Feelings (within):
Manipulation	Low self esteem
Powerlessness	Despair
Control	Hurt
Self-blaming	Guilt
Super responsibility	Shame
Protectiveness	Loneliness
Seriousness	Anger
Denial	Fear
Fragility	Rage
	Panic

Beginning therapeutic relationships with the family is important. "Acting" versus "reacting" to the defenses of family members can make all the difference. Reacting to defenses only reinforces the negative self-image and feelings and slows progress in directing the expression of the CD person's defenses and feelings in a constructive way. "Act" by knowing the characteristics of each person in the family and work with him/her accordingly through recreation activities. It will be necessary to select activities that meet the specific needs of each family member.

Leisure and recreation are essential components in the family mobile. They help maintain balance and interrelationships. Oftentimes the CD condition has caused total withdrawal by the family, leaving the CD person on his or her own. If this occurs, TR personnel should still try to involve the family, or at least a part of the family in the TR portion of the rehabilitation program. If this is not possible, then another substitute support group needs to be considered.

Family activities that can be done in inpatient, outpatient, or community programs are described in the first section below. The second section involves activities that the family can do at home.

Family Recreation Sessions

If the family is willing to get involved here are some questions that you might ask during the first session to get them to thinking about the family unit in relationship to leisure and recreation. It is best to focus on the present. It is also useful to assign homework tasks to help family members establish new interactional behavior patterns.

— What type of things does your family do together?
    Do you joke, talk at meals, go shopping together, picnic, travel?
    Do you share "happenings," good and bad?

— Who taught you the leisure skills that you now have?

— Think about your parents, do they like and do the same kind of things you do?

— What are some common interests that your family shares?

181

Openers for Family Recreation Sessions

Activities (inpatient/outpatient) that could be used for openers of family recreation sessions include the following:

New Game

Each person introduces himself or herself by an activity which starts with the same letter as first or last name. Example: I am Alice, and I like aerobics.

Scavenger Hunt

Make a list of experiences that people in the group might have had. Give each person a copy of the list and have them try to find people who fit the experiences.

Lineups

Have group line up according to height, while having eyes closed. When they think they have the line, let them open eyes. Take a minute to have persons speak to other people on either side of them.

Another way to play this game is to have people line up according to birthdays, without speaking.

Who Am I?

Name of a different cartoon character or TV personality (or whatever might be appropriate) is placed on each person's back as he or she enters the room. Person cannot see what the name is. Must ask questions of other persons to determine who he or she is.

Rope Map

The group makes a map of the United States by outlining it with a long rope (map must be large enough to hold all participants). Ask people to go to (1) place where they were born; (2) place where they had the best vacation; and (3) place where they would like to live. At each place, ask the persons something about it.

Trust: Car

One person is the car (decides kind and color). Sponsor is the driver. The car cannot see (person keeps eyes closed, or use blindfold). Driver puts hands on shoulders of "car" and guides car through the building, or in the outdoors, by giving verbal directions. Driver tries to be creative, e.g., "You are in two lane traffic, car coming up behind you." Change places and take a different route.

Trust Fall

Two persons from family work as a team. One person stands one foot behind the other person. Front person falls backwards, with the back person catching him or her. Faller moves forward six inches, and again falls back.

This takes lots of trust in the other person. If there is a big difference in size, have the larger person get on his or her knees, both for falling and for catching.

Hug Tag

One person is IT and carries a sponge paddle, which is used to tag another person, who then becomes IT. In order to avoid being tagged, persons must hug another person (or grasp their elbows). After the game gets in full swing, change the number of persons who must hug to three or four, or more (depending on number in the group).

Parachute Play

Use a 12 foot parachute. Have people grasp the edges and lift it up in the air and then let it settle down. Variations: (1) Have people wearing something blue change places (running under the parachute) while the parachute is up. (2) All people who like to swim, change places. (3) Do the Bunny Hop, holding edge of parachute. Think of other things that could be done, or ask participants for suggestions.

Goofy Olympics

Set up a bunch of different stations. Have each family as a team. Activities which might be included: water balloon toss, 3-legged race, potato sack race, tricycle race, spoon and egg relay, water in a cup relay, balloon pop relay, jump rope contest, and pie eating contest.

Sequences

Everyone is in a circle. One person throws a ball to someone else in the circle and then puts hand on shoulder. Person who receives it, passes it to someone else, and puts hand on shoulder. This continues until everyone has received the ball (hand on shoulder indicates you have had the ball and cannot receive it again). The trick here is that you must remember to whom you pass and from whom you received the ball. Follow the same sequence again only faster.

Add another ball of different size or color, so both balls are following the same path. Another challenge is to reverse the route of the ball, so you pass it to person from whom you received it.

Nature Hunt

Hand out a list of 10 nature items to each family. Family works together to find articles on list. Set a time limit of 30 minutes on this, at which time each family displays what they have found.

BLINDMAN'S SEARCH

<u>Category:</u> Family Activity
<u>Supplies:</u> Objects such as tennis ball, cone
<u>Age Level:</u> Family
<u>Time:</u> 10 minutes
<u>Objectives:</u>   To have the family work together as one unit
                    To use verbal communication effectively
                    To have fun

<u>Description/Instructions:</u> Line up families facing the leader. Select one person from each family to be blindfolded. After they are blindfolded, place an object out in front of each line about 100 yards away. Instruct the families that they are to lead the blindfolded person to the object by verbally instructing them from their line. The blindfolded person is to be led down past the object, about 10 yards past, and then is to spin around three times. Then, the search begins! The family members need to give verbal directions until the object is found. Remind the families to be encouraging, even if they are laughing hysterically! After all, they are the ones directing.

FAMILY PIZZA

<u>Category:</u> Family/Self-Esteem
<u>Supplies:</u> For each family or group, one large circle 2 feet in diameter cut out of white paper, scissors, chairs, table, tape, markers
<u>Age Level:</u> Family, children, adult
<u>Time:</u> 40 - 50 minutes
<u>Objectives:</u>   To identify unique and positive aspects about one's self
                    To improve self-esteem
                    To increase self-awareness and awareness of family members

<u>Description/Instructions:</u> The activity begins with the above listed supplies being distributed among the family and/or client groups. The families or groups are asked to cut a slice out of their pizza, one for each person so that all of the pizza is gone (some pieces may be larger than others). The groups or families are further instructed to draw, but not color in, on their slice all the toppings that they like on their pizza, large enough so that a word can be printed inside. The families or groups are further asked to draw a crust on the pizza and put their names within the crust.

Once all have finished drawing, the families or groups are then asked to write a different positive aspect about themselves within each topping. When all have completed their slice of pizza by filling in all their toppings, they tape their pizza back together on the wall. If the clients or family members are not able to fill in all or any of the toppings with positive aspects about themselves, they are still instructed to put their slice up on the wall so that their pizza is completed.

When the pizza pies are completed, each member of the family or group is asked to step forth individually and read to the group those positive aspects that they listed about themselves. For those clients or family members who did not complete their pizza with positive aspects the activity leader asks their group or family to give positive aspects they see in that person. These are then placed on the pizza.

Processing: It is important to possess positive aspects about ourselves. Relationships begin with liking ourselves first and then liking others.

Families or client groups are better able to function, understand, and get along when we know and share positive things about ourselves.

It is okay to share our unique qualities and it isn't considered bragging if we do it appropriately and within reason.

For those groups or family members who could not identify positive aspects about themselves: these aspects can be developed through recreation, socialization, communication, hobbies, volunteering, etc., and having them is an important part in everyone's life.

CREATE YOUR OWN GAME

Category: Family
Supplies: Boxes, filled with all types of balls, bats, bean bags, frisbees, ropes, etc.
Age Level: Adolescent, adult, family
Time: 50 minutes
Objectives: To develop creativity
To develop cooperation
To have family create and play together

Description/Instructions: Each family (or group) selects a box full of props. Each family "invents" a game that uses all the props in the box. Each family then introduces the game to others, who join in playing it.

Processing: What did you think of the games?
Was it hard to "create" a game?
Did everyone cooperate and come up with ideas?
Did you have fun?
Will you play this game again?

LEISURE SCRABBLE

Category: Family
Supplies: 1" x 1" cards with a letter of alphabet on each, paper, pencil for each family
Age Level: Family
Time: 20 - 30 minutes
Objectives: To work as a team
To provide positive competitive game
To develop a resource of activities for family
To have fun as a family

Description/Instructions: Turn "Scrabble" cards face down. Leader flips over a card and calls out the letter. Each family, who has designated one member to write, has one minute to write down all the leisure activities they can think of that begin with that letter. Then the recorder from each family calls out the list, which must be approved as leisure activities by the other families. Leader then flips over another card. Total up the number of leisure activities for each team. If the same letter comes up a second time, each team must list all activitiees which contain that letter (not begin with that letter).

185

FINGERPAINT A MOOD

<u>Category:</u> Family/Arts and Crafts
<u>Supplies:</u> Various colors of fingerpaint, large white paper, music: classical, rock, country
<u>Age Level:</u> Adolescent, adult
<u>Time:</u> 30 minutes
<u>Objectives:</u>　　To express creativity through drawing and music
　　　　　　　　　To get to know family members in another dimension

<u>Description/Instructions:</u> Each person has a large space on table and access to several colors of fingerpaint. Follow these instructions:

1. Listen to this classical music. Close your eyes and try to feel the mood of the music. Fingerpaint your mood and feelings.

2. Listen to this rock music. Feel the mood of this music also. Fingerpaint your mood and feelings.

3. Listen to this country music. Feel the mood of this music. Fingerpaint your mood and feelings.

4. List three feelings while you painted to the classical music.

5. List three feelings while you painted to rock music.

6. List three feelings while you painted to country music.

7. Do you see painting and/or music as ways of relaxing?

8. Which type of music did you find more relaxing?

9. Did the type of music affect the colors you chose to use?

10. If you posted your fingerpaintings, could another person tell which was done to classical, to rock, to country? Try it out.

Family Interests and Activities That Can Be Done at Home

Besides the inpatient, outpatient, and community activities for families, it is important to work with people to determine what they are like and what they can do at home. Following are a few activities and suggestions.

FAMILY ESTEEM INVENTORY

Instructions: Mentally insert the name of the person being evaluated in the blank space. Put your evaluation in the right hand column. Rating can be a simple yes-no or a scale from 1 to 5. It can be used by clients, with or without the assistance of TR staff, and by all family members.

Rating

1. _____ will sit down with someone and encourage him or her to talk informally. _____

2. _____ is sensitive to another who is discouraged, restless, troubled, or silent. _____

3. _____ interrupts others when they are talking. _____

4. _____ compliments individuals about things they do. _____

5. _____ shows warmth and affection. _____

6. _____ frequently nags others. _____

7. _____ acts as though he or she is listening to a person when he or she really is not. _____

8. _____ asks others' opinion about things he or she would like to do, receive, etc. _____

9. _____ is sarcastic. _____

10. _____ tries to see another's point of view. _____

11. _____ enjoys listening to family members. _____

12. _____ monopolizes conversation. _____

13. _____ encourages others to share their thoughts, feelings, convictions without criticizing them . _____

14. _____ is able to speak the truth in a loving manner. _____

15. _____ gets upset or defensive when others disagree with him or her. _____

16. _____ gives many orders, commands, and directions to family members. _____

17. _____ talks positive about other family members. _____

Source: Unknown

FAMILY ACTIVITIES SHEET

ACTIVITY/INTEREST	WHICH FAMILY MEMBERS NOW PARTICIPATE?	HOW COULD THIS ACTIVITY BE DEVELOPED?
BREAKFAST		
LUNCH		
DINNER		
READING		
CAMPING		
GARDENING		
COOKING		
HOBBIES		
OUTDOOR GAMES		
SPECTATOR SPORTS		
FAMILY EVENING		
TABLE GAMES		

Activities for Family to Do Together

Caring and Sharing as a Family Unit
> Physical activities -- walking, swimming, bowling
> Picnics
> Meal time

Communication
> Telling of something good that happened
> Expressing how you feel
> Giving "warm fuzzies" -- complimenting someone
> Setting a time each day for the family to communicate

Sharing Your Talents
> Do something in which you are good, e.g., make a gourmet dish, teach a family member
> > a card trick
> Each person makes a special dish for dinner -- draw numbers to see what is served first

Family Projects
> Garden -- flower, vegetables, or rock garden
> Holiday -- build things, plan trip
> Pets
> Make and play homemade games

Outdoors
> Look at stars -- identify the stars and constellations
> Identify birds -- make a bird feeder
> Fish, hunt
> Camp, hike
> Bike, jog
> Explore in a city or state park
> Swim, games in the pool
> Barbecue
> Backyard games -- badminton, frisbee, croquet, horseshoes, boccie, kick the can,
> > sardines, steal the flag, jacks, marbles
> Neighborhood get-together
> Garage sales

Car Games
> Sing
> Identify license plates -- count number from each state
> Identify make of cars
> Read unusual signs

Indoor Activities
> Table games -- riddles, tic-tac-toe, Trivial Pursuits, Pictionary, Monopoly
> Card games
> Photography
> Storytelling, poetry

Family Esteem Building

Honor Day

Plan one day during which a family member is honored. Plan a special meal of his or her choice. Family members creatively express appreciation for this family member through art, music, etc. May be planned on a monthly basis.

What I Did Well Today

May be included as table conversation or as a part of an evening together. Each family member shares what he or she did that day which felt good. Encourages persons to feel good about themselves.

Family Shield

Family designs its own shield or coat of arms. May include: family verse, symbol of greatest strength, three words to remember family, symbol of each family member. (See Coat of Arms.)

What I Appreciate About . . .

Choose one family member. Other family members share one thing they appreciate about that person. Then go to the second family member, etc. May want to post responses as visual reminder.

A variation of this is to cut out a circle from construction paper. Put a smaller circle in center with family member's name. Other family members write in what they appreciate about that person.

Family Letters or Notes

Family members can send letters to other family members expressing appreciation. Parental example teaches chldren to speak well of others.

20 Ways to Say I Love You

Brainstorm 20 ways to say "love you" to family members. Each family member chooses one way to express his/her love that week.

Compliment Chart

Family members brainstorm things for which to compliment people. Complete list in form of a chart. Whenever a family member receives a compliment, he/she writes complimentor's name on the chart.

COAT OF ARMS

<u>Instructions:</u> Each family member will make his or her coat of arms and then share it with family.

1. Represent the most enjoyable leisure activity that you do by yourself.
2. Draw your favorite activity you do with your family.
3. What do you like to do best with your friends?
4. If you had a year off with no responsibilities, what would you do?
5. What is a leisure activity you've never done that you would like to try?
6. What is your motto about fun, leisure, play, etc.?

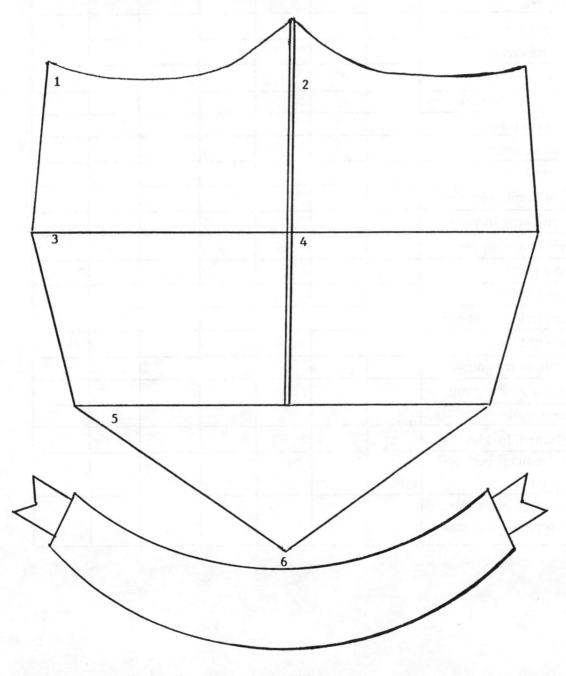

191

ENRICHING FAMILY TIME

Instructions: Plan family activities that you would like to do this week. Put the initials of family members who will share in this activity in the appropriate box. Post the sheet in a conspicuous place to serve as a reminder.

ACTIVITY	SUN	MON	TUES	WED	THURS	FRI	SAT
Play games							
Camp out							
Fishing trip							
Sing together							
Go get ice cream							
Read book together							
Everyone helps cook							
Go on bike hike							
Eat out							
Visit family friends							
Look at family pictures							
Do something in yard							
Go window-shopping							
Go on a picnic							
Go swimming							
Watch choice TV show							
Make a gift together							
Play miniature golf							
Play cards/table game							
Go for a walk							
Give "warm fuzzies"							
Organize neighborhood picnic/party							
Talk about a good thing that happened that day							

PLANNING GUIDE FOR THE FAMILY

FAMILY MEMBERS INVOLVED _____

_____

DATE OF GOAL SETTING _____

FAMILY GOALS (rank in order of importance)

1. _____

_____

DATE TO BE ACHIEVED _____

ACTIVITY IDEAS _____

2. _____

_____

DATE TO BE ACHIEVED _____

ACTIVITY IDEAS _____

3. _____

_____

DATE TO BE ACHIEVED _____

ACTIVITY IDEAS _____

4. _____

_____

DATE TO BE ACHIEVED _____

ACTIVITY IDEAS _____

BIWEEKLY REVIEW

1. _____

_____

2. _____

_____

3. _____

_____

REFERENCES

Alcoholics Anonymous. (1976). *Alcoholics Anonymous (3rd ed.)*. New York, NY: Al-Anon World Services, Inc. "Twelve Steps of Alcoholics Anonymous," p. 59.

Artz, B. (nd). *Ideas are the heart of the program*. Alexandria, VA: National Recreation and Park Association. "Polaroid Scavenger Hunt," p. 33.

Barksdale, L.S. (1980). Personal stress evaluation. Idyllwild, CA: The Barksdale Foundation. "Self Esteem.

Brennan, J. (1981). *Memories, dreams, and thoughts: A guide to mental stimulation*. Washington, D.C.: American Health Care Association. "Famous Numbers"," p. 105-110; "Occupations," p. 7; "Music," p. 137-141.

Bullock, C., and Palmer, R. *Recreation - the time of your life*. Chapel Hills, NC: University of North Carolina, Recreation Administration Department. "Leisure Activity Motivators," p. 8; "Leisure Alternatives Worksheet," p. 34.

Drugs in Perspective. (Trainer and Participant Manuals.) (1979). Washington, DC: National Drug Abuse Center. "How Do You Cope," p. 150-154.

Earle, P. (1981). *Leisure education notebook for community alcohol programs*. Eugene, OR: Eugene Parks and Recreation Department. "Leisure Activity Self Contract," p. 65.

Faulkner, R. (1991). Therapeutic recreation protocal for treatment of substance addictions. State College, PA: Venture Publishing, Inc. "Balanceform," p. 138.

Floyd, K., and Negely, S. (1989). *I believe in me* (Project I.B.M.). Salt Lake City, UT: The Western Institute of Neuropsychiatry, University of Utah.

Graber, S. (1987). *Drugs of abuse*. Kalispell, MT: Scott Publishing Company. "Controlled Substances: Uses and effects," p. 16-17.

Guzman, H. (1991). Unpublished worksheets. [Needs Assessment]. Central Michigan University Recreation and Park Administration Department. "Send Up the Message"; "See It - Believe It."

Howe, L. (1977). *Taking charge of your life*. Miles, IL: Argus Communications. "Validation Scavenger Hunt," p. 24.

Johnson, C. (1991). Road to recovery. *Therapeutic Recreators in Recovery*, January. p. 2.

Karapetian, D. (nd). Chelsea Community Hospital, Kresge House. "Leisure Assessment."

Korb, K., Azok, S., and Leutenberg, E. (1989). *Life managememt skills*. Beachwood, OH: Wellness Reproductions, Inc. "One Step at a Time," p. 15; "No Man Is an Is-Land," p. 43; "Exercise Interest Checklist," p. 4.

Maslow, A. (1962). *Toward a psychology of being*. Princeton, NJ: D. Van Nostrand Co. p. 463.

McDowell, C. (1976). *Leisure counseling: Selected lifestyle processes*. Eugene, OR: Center of Leisure Studies, University of Oregon. "Pie of Life," p. 84; "Open ended questions related to Leisure Values," p. 131-133.

McDowell, C. (1983). *Leisure wellness: Concepts and helping strategies*. (nine booklets). Eugene, OR: Sun Moon Press. Leisure wellness: An introduction #1. Leisure Wellness: Concepts & Principles #2. Leisure wellness: Intimate relationships #3. Leisure wellness: Identity & social roles #4. Leisure wellness: Strategies for fitness #5. Leisure wellness: Assessing your leisure style & formulating strategies #6, "Leisure Lifestyle Inventory," p. 20. Leisure wellness: Coping strategies & managing stress #7. Leisure wellness: Coping strategies and managing stress #7. Leisure wellness: Managing Economics, time & cultural forces #9.

Murphy, J. (1975). *Recreation and leisure services:* A humanistic approach. Dubuque, IA: Wm. C. Brown Company.

O'Connor, C. (1986). *Lifestyling: Lifestyle stress management systems.* Chico, CA: Connie O'Connor. "Whole Person Stress Inventory," p. 7; "Buffers," p. 8; "4-Star Buffers," p. 15.

O'Dea-Evans, P. (1990). *LEAP workshop.* Algonquin, IL: Pea Pod Publications. "LEAP Assessment," p. 2-8.

O'Dea-Evans, P. (1991). *Leisure education for addicted persons.* Algonquin, IL: Pea Pod Publications. "Individual Barrier List," p. 28; "Barriers," p. 45.

O'Dea-Evans, P. (1988). *Self disclosure and team building activities for chemical dependency and prevention groups.* Algonquin, IL: Therapeutic Recreators for Recovery. "Record Album Cover," p. 25; "That Was Then, This Is Now," p. 34.

Peterson, C., and Gunn, S. (1984). *Therapeutic recreation program design: Principles and procedures* (2d ed.) Englewood Cliffs, NJ: Prentice-Hall, Inc.

Phelps, D. (1989). Outdoor adventures in recovery. Therapeutic Recreators for Recovery newsletter, December. "Outdoor Adventures in Recovery," p. 2.

Rainwater, A., and Guzman, H. (1991). Contradictions between needs, feelings, and behaviors or the chemically dependent person. Unpublished paper, Central Michigan University.

Recreation Therapy Department, Chelsea Community Hospital, Chelsea, MI. Leisure Assessment and Initial Treatment Plan.

Rice, W., and Yaconelli, M. (1986). *Play it.* Grand Rapids, MI: Zondervan Publishing House. "Musical Costumes," p. 124.

Riley, B., and Newman, I. (1982). *Decisions about alcohol and other drugs: A curriculum for Nebraska schools.* Lincoln, NE: University of Nebraska-Lincoln (NCPADA). "Decision Making Process," p. 13-16;"Steps in Decision Making," p. 19; "Consequence Sheet," p. 29.

Rohnke, K. (1977). *Cowstails and cobras.* Hamilton, MA: Project Adventure, Inc.

Rohnke, K. (1989). *Cowstails and cobras II.* Dubuque, IA: Kendall/Hunt Publishing Co. "Moonball," p. 60; "The Wave, or Butt Off," p. 65; "Frisalevio," p. 71.

Rohnke, K. (1974). *Project Adventure.* Hamilton, MA: Project Adventure, Inc.

Rohnke, K. (1984). *Silver bullets: A guide to initiative problems, adventure games and trust activities.* Hamilton, MA: Project Adventure, Inc.

Rush, L. (1991). Laughter and play. *Addiction and Recovery.*,March/April.

Schoel, J., Prouty, D., and Radcliffe, P. (1988). *Islands of healing: A guide to adventure based counseling.* Hamilton, MA: Project Adventure, Inc. "Personal Responsibility Activities," p. 293; "Communication Activities," p. 287; "Ice Breakers/Acquaintance Activities," p. 281; "De-Inhibitizer Activities," p. 283; "Social Responsibility Activities," p. 291; "Decision Making/Problem Solving Activities," p. 289; "Trust Activities," p. 285.

Simmons, G.A., and Cannon, E.C. (1991). *It is outdoors: A guide to experiential activities.* Reston, VA: American Alliance for Health, Physical Education, Recreation and Dance.

Simon, S.B., Howe, L.W., and Kirschenbaum, H. (1972). *Values clarification: A handbook of practical strategies for teachers and students.* New York, NY: Hart Publishing, Co., Inc. "Twenty Things I Love to Do," p. 30.

Stumbo, N., and Thompson, S. (1986). *Leisure education: A manual of activities and resources.* State College, PA: Venture Publishing, Inc. "Leisure Coat of Arms" (adapted). p. 76.

Wegschneider, S. (1979). From family trap to family freedom. *Alcoholism,* Jan/Feb. pp. 36-37.

Watson, John (nd). *Recreation assessment worksheet)* Huron Oaks, Ann Arbor, MI.

Witman, J., Kurtz, J., and Nichols, S. (1987). *Reflections, recognition, reaffirmation: A frame of reference for leisure education including activities, techniques, and resources.* Hamstead, NH: Hamstead Hospital. "Career Choice" (adapted), p. 58; "Stress Problem Solving," p. 81; "A Potpourri of Goals" (adapted), p. 39.

Zackson, F. (1986). Lifestyle rehabilitation: The second recovery track. *Alcohol, Health and Research World,* Fall, p. 70

ADDITIONAL RESOURCES

Duquette, M. (1987). *Leisure education program starter.* Arlington, VA: Michael Duquette.

Fitts, W. (1970). *Interpersonal competence: The wheel model* (booklet). Nashville, TN: Counselor Recording and Press.

Godbey, S. (1985). *Leisure in your life: An exploration* (2d ed.). State College, PA: Venture Publishing, Inc.

Hoper, C., Kutzlab, U., Stobbe, A., and Weber, B. (1975). *Awareness games: Personal growth through group interaction.* New York, NY: St. Martin's Press.

Lawson, G., Ellis, D., and Rivers, P. (1984). *Essentials of chemical dependency counseling.* Rockville, MD: Aspen Publishing Co., Aspen Systems Corporation.

Mundy, J. and Odum, L. (1987). *Leisure education: Theory and practice.* New York, NY: John Wiley & Sons.

Pearse, J. (1981). *Clouds on the clothesline and 200 other great games.* Huntsville, Ontario, Canada: Camp Tawingo Publications.

Weinstein, M. and Goodman, J. (1980). *Playfair.* San Luis Obispo, CA: Impact Publishers.